W9-AVE-705

# The Writer
# in the Jewish Community

SARA F. YOSELOFF MEMORIAL PUBLICATIONS
In Judaism and Jewish Affairs


This volume is one in a series established in memory
of Sara F. Yoseloff,
who devoted her life to the making of books.

# The Writer
# in the Jewish Community

## An Israeli–North American
## Dialogue

Edited by
# Richard Siegel and Tamar Sofer

Rutherford ● Madison ● Teaneck
Fairleigh Dickinson University Press
London and Toronto: Associated University Presses

Associated University Presses
440 Forsgate Drive
Cranbury, NJ 08512

Associated University Presses
25 Sicilian Avenue
London WC1A 2QH, England

Associated University Presses
P.O. Box 338, Port Credit
Mississauga, Ontario
Canada L5G 4L8

The paper used in this publication meets the requirements of the American National Standard for Permanence of Paper for Printed Library Materials Z39.48-1984.

**Library of Congress Cataloging-in-Publication Data**

The Writer in the Jewish community: an Israeli–North American dialogue / edited by Richard Siegel and Tamar Sofer.
    p.   cm.
  Includes index.
  ISBN 0-8386-3459-1
  1. Israel and the diaspora—Congresses.   2. American literature—Jewish authors—Congresses.   3. Authors, Israeli—Congresses.
4. Jews—United States—Identity—Congresses.   5. Israel—Intellectual life—Congresses.   I. Siegel, Richard, 1947–   .
II. Sofer, Tamar.
DS132.W75   1993
973'.04924—dc20
                                                    91-58951
                                                    CIP

PRINTED IN THE UNITED STATES OF AMERICA

# Contents

# Foreword

## Eli Shaltiel

The end of the nineteenth century saw a massive and revolutionary metamorphosis in the history of the Jewish people. Historians and sociologists were quick to identify the external causes that shook the Jewish people and radically changed its image. Those who thought that the problems and hardships of the Jewish people sprung from the fact that they existed "outside history," were not surprised to find that the transformations taking place in the society surrounding them caused such dramatic changes in the character, structure, and future of a people who were not masters of their fate. The most manifest and acute transformation was no doubt the rapid mass emigration of Jews from their traditional centers to the New World. Of course, this radical demographic process had long-lasting effects on the ways of life of the Jewish people. Traditions centuries old were shattered, new and exciting ideas were conquering new hearts and minds. The nationalist revival was only one of the aspects of this revolutionary process, and only few chose the national solution as a means to escape their difficult straits. The masses chose the individual solution, the saving of life and the maintaining of existence, but there were those few who reached the conclusion that there can be no individual solution without a collective one. Reviving the Hebrew language and adapting it to the needs of a developing and modern world was one of the first indications of the Jewish renaissance—in the Zionist movement and in the movements preceding it. Reading Hebrew journals, the encouragement and dissemination of literary works in the reviving language, were tangible and prominent aspects of the identification with this new and radical development. The option to create a dramatic change through uprisings and diplomacy, which other national movements had, was not available to the Jewish people, and when tried a few times, only brought disappointment. The revived Hebrew, which expanded and gained new terrain daily, was a rare proof of the validity of the vision, which many skeptics and realists considered just another Messianic mirage of the kind so prolific throughout the history of the Jewish people.

Even today, after more than a century of vigorous national endeavor, and more than forty years since the realization of the vision of Jewish sovereignty, there are still those who question the fundamental theses of the Zionist idea. Has the State of Israel indeed served as a solution to the distress and agony of the Jews in the modern world? Has assimilation been halted? Has the fact that the Jewish people are no longer guests living among other people, but can now play host in their own country had a fundamental impact on them? The balance between positive and negative answers, between great expectations and great disappointments is not at all clear-cut or unequivocal. In the table charting the achievements and failures one column depicts amazing and great achievements. The revivification of the Hebrew language is a rare and unique endeavor, probably unparalleled in the history of mankind. Through times of uncertainty and distress, when doubts and despair raised trenchant enquiries about the price paid for the way chosen, the Hebrew language remained a unifying and uplifting element. Conserving and nurturing it, cultivating and disseminating it, it unites Israelis who cannot agree on any other point. In an era searching for signs of uniqueness and communal existence, rejecting one after the other any solutions offered to it, the shared past and the Hebrew language remain the uniting and bracing forces that time and its permutations cannot vanquish. Its subjects have changed, its focal points have shifted, but the role of Hebrew literature and the status it holds in the heart of its readers have not been blemished.

In his criticism of the arguments raised by Ted Solotaroff concerning the status of American Jewish literature today, Irving Howe argues that the North American Jewish writers are going through "a crisis of subject-matter." It would seem that Israeli writers do not suffer the same straits. Many of them complain of the alienation of the political establishment, all of them bemoan the demanding covenant they have with a language whose readership is so small and limited. Some are quite convinced that a prejudice against the State of Israel and the Jewish people precludes them from becoming Nobel Laureates. But they are not short of material. The Hebrew writer, by the sheer fact of writing, and many a time without being conscious of his enterprise, became one of the key elements of the renewal and restoration of the Hebrew language. In this heady atmosphere even the writing of a lyrical poem had national significance. The new Hebrew literature was unique in that it never avoided the acute issues of national existence. The Russian writers of the nineteenth century dealt time and again, as if in a trance, with the "cursed questions" of Russian existence; the Hebrew writers, who were strongly influenced by the Russian, once repeatedly asked "where to?," how and why, who are we and what is our destiny. In typical Jewish practice, which contrived to interpret the "Song of Songs" as the description of the relations between the children of Israel and the Divine Presence, so did the contemporary readers of Hebrew literature manage to detect in any item of Hebrew writing the debates and misgivings of the times. Even a simple and touching story about the history of a Jewish family was closely scrutinized and examined for its contribution to the clarification of the problem of Jewish identification and the Israeli nature of our time.

Quite often the Israeli readers search the literature they read for answers to the questions the politicians evade. Many trenchant discussions on the nature of the Arab-Israeli conflict or a heart-searching debate on the significance of the Holocaust and the nature of the relationship between Israel and the Diaspora arise from the reading of important literary works. It seems as if a society that energetically avoids a realistic and penetrating discussion of its existential situation, is recalled time and again by its writers to deliberate its tortuous condition.

The writers' conference in Berkeley seemingly brought together two groups whose differences were more numerous than the uniting and binding factors. But it was clear that there was a willingness to reach a mutual understanding and to define the points of agreement. The meeting might not have supplied an exact definition of the nature of Jewish literature in our time, but the participants left Berkeley with the feeling that Jewish literature with its many languages still has a devoted and loyal readership. The Jewish writer was not shorn of his or her traditional role, whose exact definition is not definite, and whose demands are taxing and exacting.

It seems that all the Israeli writers emphasized, in one way or another, their affinity with the Hebrew language as the linchpin joining them in an unbreakable bond to the people's past and to their own identity. They implied that they expected the other participants to cultivate the language in their own surroundings. The involvement of the American Jewish writers in the affairs of the State of Israel, and their willingness to express decided opinions on its internal affairs, its behavior and future, are unmistakable evidence of the mutual responsibility still strongly felt. The speeches of the participants, as can be seen in this book, reflect the feeling of a partnership in a shared destiny, an indefinable relationship at times, but even so an everlasting one, to which the writer has to contribute through his artistic creation.

# Introduction

## Richard Siegel

In late 1986, program staff at the National Foundation for Jewish Culture (NFJC) began discussing options for commemorating the upcoming fortieth Anniversary of the State of Israel in 1988. These discussions focused on the development of Jewish culture since the founding of the State—both in Israel and in America—and the relationship between the Jewish cultural experiences in these two dissimilar centers of contemporary Jewish life.

Fortuitously, the CRB Foundation had recently been established by philanthropist Charles R. Bronfman of Montreal with one of its main objectives to facilitate cultural interchange between Israel and the North American Diaspora. One of the main problems that the CRB Foundation identified in contemporary Jewish life was the increasing alienation between the younger generations in Israel and in the American Jewish community. Many American Jews, born after the establishment of the State of Israel, had no memory of the Holocaust or the drama of Israel's birth or even the galvanizing impact of the Six-Day War. Many Israelis, also born after the establishment of the State, disdained the American Jewish community as a vestige of the galut (exile) experience, and had difficulty recognizing the cultural validity of the American Jewish experience.

In this environment, the common bonds and ideals of these two centers of Jewish life were becoming obscured. Without active intervention, the distancing process would continue to the ultimate detriment and weakening of both communities—politically, socially, and culturally.

Recognizing that this was essentially a cultural situation—reflecting a common cultural heritage, yet competing contemporary experiences—the CRB Foundation brought the National Foundation for Jewish Culture together with cultural agencies in Israel to jointly plan a series of programs designed to analyze these dynamics and stimulate greater cultural understanding between the two centers of contemporary Jewish life.

11

The rationale for this project, entitled "Independence and Inter-dependence: Israel-North America Cultural Exchange," was articulated in its public program materials:

> For forty years, North American Jewry has joined with Israel in the awesome and inspiring tasks of nation-building. Forty years is a biblical generation, and a new generation is emerging both within Israel and in the Diaspora which seeks to infuse a new spirit of partnership into the creation of contemporary Jewish culture.

> "Independence and Interdependence: Israel-North America Cultural Exchange" explores that realm of the spirit which the arts inhabit. Through the media of music, literature, dance and theater, artists can express and audiences can share their diverse experiences and visions as Jews in the modern world. In the programs of "Independence and Inter-dependence," the arts are presented as vehicles for communication and understanding for a People bound together by a common Jewish history and destiny, although separated by contemporary experience.

While all of the programs presented through "I&I"—including performance tours, arts residencies, and festivals—made valuable contributions to the dialogue, either in furthering intercultural understanding or in raising new questions, the three, three-day cultural conferences held in the United States have had the most sustained impact, both on the participants and on the intellectual dialogue. "Memory and Creativity: Jewish Tradition in the Performing Arts" was held in Philadelphia in May 1988; "The Writer in the Jewish Community: An Israeli-North American Dialogue" was held in the San Francisco Bay Area in October 1988; and "Counter-Harmonies: The Jewish Experience in Music in the 20th Century" was held in New York in April 1989.

Of the three, "The Writer in the Jewish Community" involved the most intricate planning—defining the issues, identifying the participants, structuring the discussions. Eli Shaltiel, then Senior Editor at Am Oved Publishers, was the Israeli chairman, and Robert Alter, Chairman of the Department of Comparative Literature at UC-Berkeley, was the American chair. Together with the American and Israeli Executive Producers of "I&I," they identified the themes: Jewish identity and the literary imagination; the problematics of writing within the two societies; and the relationship between the Israeli and American Jewish literary communities.

The structure of this anthology reflects these themes, rather than the specific conference sessions. As such, it is not a publication of proceedings recording all of the presentations or covering all of the issues discussed at the conference.

Part I: "The Jew as Writer/The Writer as Jew" includes personal statements by both Israeli and American participants reflecting deeply individual perspectives on Jewish identity and its impact on the literary process. Part II: "Jewish Writing in Context" looks at issues that Jewish writers are dealing with respectively in America and in Israel. Part III: "Breaking the Language Barrier: Literary Dialogues between Israel and the Diaspora" begins to explore the potential and problematics of the literary relationship between Israel and the North American Diaspora.

Eli Shaltiel's "Forword" and Nessa Rapoport's "Afterword" provide personal reflections on the conference and its impact from the Israeli and American perspectives respectively.

It should be noted that among the papers not included in this anthology are a number that comment on the interplay of literature and politics, particularly in the Israeli context. The conference was not intended to deal with this issue; in fact, it was designed to try to limit this discussion. Given the politicized nature of the literary community in Israel and the passionate debate about Israel within the American intellectual community, it was inevitable that political discussions would emerge. However, the conference was meant to focus on issues of literature and identity, not policies of the Israeli government, and a number of participants would only agree to attend if the agenda were nonpolitical.

As it turned out, several participants did raise provocative questions about the role and responsibility of the writer in the political environment. The debate continued after the conference, in fact, in various newspapers and journals both in Israel and the United States. These discussions are not reflected in this anthology. They could not be presented accurately without including the subsequent debates, and their inclusion would have distorted both the essence of the conference and the focus of this anthology.

"The Writer in the Jewish Community: An Israeli-North American Dialogue" provided a context to explore cultural relationships between Israel and the North American Diaspora through the perspectives of some of the most noted and gifted writers in each community. This anthology has been compiled in the hopes of continuing the dialogue. The papers that follow probe various dimensions of the relationship. However, two perspectives—one Israeli, one American—deserve particular comment because they permeated virtually every discussion.

## Language

English is the lingua franca of the Jewish world. There was no "communication" problem at the conference; everyone was more or less comfortable speaking in English. In fact, in the one session where simultaneous translation was arranged, three of the four Israeli panelists preferred speaking in English, trusting their own language skills over those of the professional translator hired for this purpose.

However, there was a problem with the symbolic nature of language. English is not a Jewish language; Hebrew is. The Israeli participants presented a sharp challenge to the American writers: If they are serious about engaging Israeli culture and nurturing contemporary Jewish culture, then they must become more serious about learning Hebrew.

Hebrew is the major cultural achievement of modern Israel. It is a reflection of the values, history, traditions, wanderings, and longings that underlie the State. Its grammar, nuances, and resonances are the materials with which Israeli writers and poets weave their stories and songs. It reacts on them and they react on it. The language is alive; it grows with each use, addition, coinage, allusion, and word play. Hebrew is the substratum of Israeli creativity and, as the language of the Jewish State, the substratum of Jewish creativity.

## Religion

Religion in Israel has become polarized and politicized between the Orthodox and the secular. Judaism in America, reflecting the religious pluralism of American society, represents a spectrum of identifications and practices ranging from secular to Orthodox.

Religious motivations and impulses are central to much of American Jewish writing, even for writers who do not consider themselves "religious" or observant. The counterpoint of the Jewish calendar and life-cycle, the language and melodies of prayer, the texts of Jewish tradition, serve to inform a distinct Jewish identity within American society and nurture American Jewish creativity.

The challenge that the American Jewish writers presented to their Israeli counterparts was to recognize the potential of creative inspiration emanating from Jewish religious traditions, rituals, and texts. This recognition could both address the politicization of religion in Israel and facilitate Israeli understanding of the central dynamic of American Jewish culture.

Now at some distance and remove from the conference, the perspectives articulated in this anthology are still challenging and provocative. "The Writer in the Jewish Community" reflects both the partnership and conflict between Israel and North American Jewry in constructing a contemporary Jewish culture. As such, it both participates in and contributes to the healthy symbiosis between these two centers of Jewish life.

Many people were instrumental in realizing the conference and anthology on "The Writer in the Jewish Community: An Israeli-North American Dialogue." As cochairs, Eli Shaltiel and Robert Alter defined the issues and shaped the contours of the discussions. Marilyn Yolles, as host, and Carolyn Steinberg, as coordinator, created a dynamic and nurturing environment for the conference.

Undertaken as part of "Independence and Interdependence: Israel-North America Cultural Exchange," the CRB Foundation, its founder Charles R. Bronfman, and its former President Stephen P. Cohen provided the inspiration and support to pursue the intercultural dialogue. The Israeli partners—Ora Goldenberg, Yossi Frost, Yaacov Agmon, and Keshet-Cultural Promotions, Inc.—brought a spirit of cooperation throughout the project.

Other support was provided by the National Endowment for the Humanities, Division of Public Humanities Programs, the Israel Committee for the 40th Anniversary, and El Al Israel Airlines.

The Board of Directors and staff of the National Foundation for Jewish Culture nurtured this project from its inception and assured its full realization. Of particular note, are NFJC Chairman George M. Zeltzer, NFJC President and Chair of "I&I" Sandra Weiner, and "I&I" Producer David Eden. Tamar Sofer, former NFJC Director of Communications and coeditor of this anthology, has skillfully guided the preparation of the manuscript through the intricacies of international cultural relations and communications. Elaine Borsykowsky, NFJC Executive Assistant, has been of immeasurable assistance in managing the manuscript preparation and contributor contacts.

In the final analysis, this volume is a tribute to the writers who participated in "The Writer in the Jewish Community." Their willingness to engage the issues gives hope that the alienation between Israel and the North American Diaspora can be bridged through earnest dialogue and open exchange of ideas.

# The Writer
# in the Jewish Community

# Part I

## The Jew as Writer/
## The Writer as Jew

# I Write Out of an Uncreated Identity

## Harvey Shapiro

How would you define your primary identity? I write out of an uncreated identity. I write to create that identity. I write out of an uncreated identity facing an uncreated world. It is all the wind and water of before creation. My wish is to realize a world and then to enter it without confusion. Therefore, I cannot say that I write as a Jew or as an American.

From the evidence on the page I know the shock waves of my identity as a Jew never stop. The evidence tells me that I bear some hatred toward the Christian world whose language and patterns of thought make my poems possible.

In my poem "Ditty" I say:

> Where did the Jewish god go?
> Up the chimney flues.
> Who saw him go?
> Six million souls.
> How did he go?
> All so still
> As dew from the grass.

That is the way Jesus came to Mary in an anonymous poem of the fifteenth century, as dew in April that falls on the grass. That is the way God left the victims of the Holocaust in the Christian twentieth century.

Because I had been tutored by Ezra Pound's book, "An ABC of Reading," I wrote an "ABC of Culture."

> So the angel of death whistles Mozart
> (As we knew he would)
> Bicycling amid the smoke of Auschwitz,
> The Jews of Auschwitz,
> In the great museum of Western Art.

In which I seem to be saying that the concentration camp is one

21

of the pure products of Western culture, belongs in the great museum of Western art, so why should it be surprising that Mengele whistled Mozart as he biked around the camp.

There was a period after World War II when I wrote only on Jewish themes and published only in Jewish magazines and conceived of my audience as being different from that of other poets. I was making a little ghetto for myself in the spirit of Jacob Glatstein's poem, "Good Night World." Had there been in those days a real community for me to join I might well have stayed in the ghetto. But my ghetto was not real and my audience, such as it was, and mostly it wasn't, was not Jewish. And so I had to enter the dangerous world.

In what sense am I a Jew today? In no sense that would satisfy any of the rabbis of my childhood. But they had problems with their Jewishness also. One of them became the president of the United Fruit Company and ended his life by jumping out the window of a skyscraper. (His name was Blackowitz when he was my rabbi and David Black when he drove for United Fruit.) Still, when I look for clues to the Way, for a way to live in my poems, I tend to pick up first on Jewish clues (clues out of normative Jewish thought or mystical Jewish thought). I seem to notice them and think I have some tribal right to them.

I have Jewish friends who have become Buddhists. Buddhist stories and modes of perceiving are very pleasant to me, yet I haven't become a Buddhist because I'm Jewish.

Actually, I'm not Jewish. I'm a Jew. A monosyllable.

Do I feel at ease in Zion? Not at all. That may be partly because my younger brother lives there. Do I feel at home in the Diaspora? In those rare times when I feel at home at all.

It may be that what is consciously Jewish in my writing style, as against my subject matter, is not Jewish at all but urban, a tone of voice I early recognized (and wanted to imitate) in the first stories of Delmore Schwartz and the poems of Paul Goodman and Charles Reznikoff. A flatfooted lyricism that I somehow associated with city streets and Yiddish speech. It may be that what is in question is not Jewish or urban—that I am of the first generation of my family to be born here and that my growing up was beside a Yiddish-speaking shtetl grandmother. So it is the immigrants' uneasiness and not specifically a Jewish uneasiness that tells in me. Though my father was in the American army in the First World War and I was in the air force in the Second, I still marveled during the days of Vietnam war protests at those young Jews who could cut up

American flags as if this were their country. It was then I recognized how much a guest I felt here. The classic immigrant feeling.

As for my social identity as a Jew, that is partly a product of American anti-Semitism. The innocuous battles with Irish and Italian gangs of kids in my childhood and the accompanying epithets. Isolated scenes. I come back decorated from a tour of duty in Italy during World War II and visit with friends at the bar of the Yale Club, where an elderly gentleman (my age now I suppose) in waistcoat and tweed jacket holds forth on how this time when the boys come back they will keep their guns and take care of the Jews. A nut but he makes an impression, and his sentiment was not exactly foreign to the Yale campus of that day. Or now I come out of the subway at Times Square where I work and a black man raises his fist to me and says, "We're gonna get Israel." Gentle reminders. American social pathology.

As a writer, however, that social pathology works in my favor. So much of American writing comes out of its cultural pockets— the Southern writing that dominated our literature after World War II, the blue-collar lyricism of Raymond Carver, Richard Ford, and Andre Dubus today. And of course the American Jewish breakthrough of which we are perhaps the heirs and waning examples.

I began by saying that I wrote out of a need to create an identity. Nevertheless, there is a plot to many of my poems. A middle-aged man wanders about the city looking for the Way. He seems harassed by the life he leads, but he takes joy in much of what he sees—until he remembers that there is no real joy for the man who cannot figure things out. He could be a Jew.

# The Storyteller as a Jew

## David Schuetz

I would like to talk to you about how I became a Jew, perhaps how I discovered that I was a Jew, how I became a writer, and how both these things were inevitably connected.

I was born in Berlin in 1941. I did not know that I was a Jew, and, naturally, I had no idea that I was destined to be a writer in a strange foreign language called Hebrew.

For various reasons, which I shall describe later, I have only a few clear memories of those early years. Just as I could not see the future *then*, I find it hard to see the past *now*.

I grew up in a world I cannot remember, among people I cannot recall, and I spoke a language that is now for me a foreign tongue. My mother tongue—I have to think twice before forming a sentence in it.

In 1948 I found myself on a boat to Eretz Yisrael. At that time I had three pieces of information about that place: first, that there was not enough land there (in fact, I thought of bringing a piece of land with me from Germany); second, I knew there were oranges there, although I did not know what an orange was; and third, I knew that the people there spoke in a strange language and wrote backwards.

The people in charge of those waves of immigration thought that I was too young to be sent to a boarding school. Instead, they sent me together with several other young kids to a moshav, where we were adopted, so to speak, by the moshavniks.

I was sent with other children to a moshav near Netanya, to board with one of the families there. The dominant figure in my new home was a tough German-born woman whose main quality was one of self-righteousness. Yes, she was fluent in German: to my misfortune she was fluent in Hebrew and was certain she knew the best way to teach it. She saw herself as an expert in this field. Her expertise had a great influence on me.

Her skill had far-reaching consequences for me. For there I was,

24

a young boy in a foreign country, living with a lady who set very strict rules: in order to help me overcome the difficulties of a new language, which sounded like meaningless noise to my ears, she developed a simple yet extremely efficient method: accordingly, I would not be given anything unless asking for it in Hebrew. So there I was, a young boy in a strange land, subject to the rule of a strange language so that *I* should learn a strange language. If I was thirsty and wanted a glass of milk, I could not get it if I asked for it in German. However, if I could painfully come out with that mysterious sound *Ani rotse halav bevakasha,* the miracle happened, I could drink! Later on when I read "Ali Baba and the Forty Thieves," it was no surprise to me that a magic phrase like "Open Sesame" could open treasures—*Halav bevakasha* had already worked miracles for me.

I must admit that in my case her teaching method was very effective. After three unpleasant months of hesitation, fear, and almost complete silence, I opened my mouth and spoke Hebrew. At that very same I stopped speaking German. I *ceased* speaking German once and for all. I ceased to think in German, even to count in German, even to dream in German. Soon after I was almost totally unable to make any use of my mother tongue. It was as if a melody on a magnetic tape was erased, and a new one recorded over it. Here and there some old notes were left, more like background noise than any distinct sounds.

As my Hebrew became more and more fluent it began to obliterate my previous language to such a degree that it began to cloud my memories of things past, to push away into oblivion the people I once knew, the sights, the smells of my youth in that country in which I once grew up—they all seemed to fade away as I forgot my native language. Without a language to remember them by, they could not survive on their own. Every once in a while I still had some nonverbal sensations from my early childhood, but they never made up a story anymore.

Every once in a while, when I heard people talking German, something would happen to me, an eerie feeling of seeing vague images behind a curtain. But the curtain grew thicker—until it was almost opaque.

This was all very strange. In Germany, the sky above was *himmel,* and the animal that gave *milch* was *kuh.* The sky had a sound of *himmel* about it, and *himmel* had the expanse of the sky built into it. The world *milch* was not just a word. It had a special taste to it. And the white liquid that came out of *kuh* had that same taste which the world *milch* had.

Now, the Hebrew word *halav* on the other hand, had no taste at all. It was just pure sound. And as the Hebrew started to take over, I entered a totally new world. Milk, which was now called *halav,* was not the same as milk which was earlier called *milch.* It was quite different, because it had a different sound associated with it, and that sound was again associated with all kinds of other feelings and sensations.

The old words then lost their power. They became useless. Now I had to reorganize my world in another language. And everything seemed to be new, nothing was the same as it was. The new language was creating a new world order for me.

Shortly after arriving in Israel, I remember, we began to study the Bible. I was in the second grade then, still struggling to decipher these strange square letters with the dots all around them. I remember this teacher we had, the one with the deep voice, reading to us from Genesis, telling us about the chaos and the darkness and the spirit of God floating on the waters. Nothing was as clear to me as this complete darkness. Nothing was so soothing as this God, who spoke and used magical words to bring order to the world. I understood just then that there was a deep connection between the world and the words used to describe it.

The plasticity of the root system fascinated me. It gave me new powers. I could bend the words over, in order to create worlds of my own. Things that I could not achieve by force I would try to get by the use of words.

It was at that time that I fell in love with the Hebrew language, my new friend. I was intrigued by its secrets and its grammatical codes. I recall playing around with grammatical roots, amusing myself by flipping words within a sentence, swapping letters within a word—the whole flexibility of the language fascinated me. I could choose words to describe what I saw, but I could also string words together to create new images I never really saw. And once the words were there I could see them. In this world of words I was a master, an absolute monarch. I could create my own order.

But that was only a beginning. There was always more. I knew that there was magic out there, behind doors that could only be unlocked with words. I knew that certain words in certain combinations can open gates to places we cannot imagine.

Shortly after I became a storyteller. I found myself in a boarding school in some remote place in the south of the country. It was quite a violent place. I had to have something to offer in order to be accepted as one of the boys. They did not like to read but they liked to be told stories. This I could do. I read as much as I could to make sure I had enough material, but there were never enough stories. So, I mixed them together and created new stories.

I still do this now. I tell stories. To unlock some of these doors that still need magic to open. I read books in Hebrew and I write my stories in Hebrew. English, for example, refuses to let me into its secrets. And so my world remains the world of the Hebrew language.

This obsession with *words* is *Jewish*. It is the hallmark of the Jewish heritage to the world: words upon words to describe it, to tame it, to make the hidden visible. I became a real Jew when I started to see my world through words and verbal images, when I realized that we have no paintings, no sculptures, no buildings, no music, and no machines. We have words. We have the STORY.

# By the Book

## Hanoch Bartov

Most writers, like most people, are anything but Jewish. Most Jews
are not what one calls published writers. In "The Jew as Writer/The
Writer as Jew"—these two messages are implied. This roundtable is
*not* about "writer as member of the Human Race" or any other
such theme, which writers—be they Russian, Jewish American,
Chinese or Israeli—may wish to air out "as writers." Now, let me
make myself clear at the outset. I cannot see any person spending
a lifetime on such infantile, frustrating, and very often thankless
an obsession, writing stories or poems, as a Jew, as an Israeli, as
a Turk, or as anything else except as his own individual, usually
not well-rounded self. I would like to limit myself to a narrower, but
to my mind a worthwhile, fascinating theme: "The Jewish Writer as
*Jew,* in America and in Israel."

Now, when I stress the "Jewish" in "Jewish Writer," what do I
have in mind? Let me begin with a quotation from the final page
of Philip Roth's *Counterlife,* in which Zuckerman, the American
Jew in gentile London, defines the kind of Jew he now considers
himself to be:

> A Jew without Jews, without Judaism, without Zionism, without Jew-
> ishness, without a temple or an army or even a pistol, a Jew clearly
> without a home, just the object itself, like a glass or an apple.

This "Jew *without*" looks more like an abstract idea, than any
single Jew in real life, including those who inhabit many brilliant
pages in *Counterlife* and other books by Philip Roth.

When I think of being Jewish, I think of the "Jew with," the
historically and culturally distinct Jew, who, unlike the abstracted
glass or apple, needs no Geiger counter to be detected. "Jew with"
what?—with a past and a culture as well as a future and a dream;
with—until quite recently—a distinct Jewish language and a tightly
organized community, living under a very detailed legal and moral

code; a Jew who upholds both *shomer v'zocher* (keep and remember) and *achake lo b'khol yom sheyavo* (I am expecting the Messiah any day now). In short, an identity founded on long memories and a never-tiring expectation of a future paradise. In face of mortal danger to Jewish continuity, this "Jew with," the historical Jew, would sometimes perform, out of desperation, a "Salto Mortalle," from past oriented turned into future oriented.

The art of writing is not our theme. Yet, to truly understand the kind of Jew and Jewish writer I have in mind, I must underline the role fiction played as a substitute for unbearable or absent reality; of the role *history invented* played in bridging a past remembered and a future imagined.

Soon after the idea of a *Judenstadt*, a Jewish State, possessed him, in the spring of 1895, Dr. Herzl began his Zionist Diary. The first entry provides us with the key to it all:

> I have been immersed for some time now in a venture of immense proportions. I do not know if I shall live to see it accomplished. But for days and weeks now it has been filling me to beyond the limits of consciousness. . . . Its outcome is too early to assess, but my heart tells me it is magnificent, dream-like, and that I should put it down in writing—if not for others than for my own enjoyment and meditation in days to come. Or is it between these two possibilities. As Literature. If the novel (Roman) will not turn into a reality, reality may turn into a novel.
>
> The name: The Chosen Land.

In passing, Herzl did both—first he wrote the pragmatic *Judenstadt* and seven years later his utopian novel *Altneuland*.

I am tempted to mention an even earlier illustration of that same wild fantasy. In 1881 the Jewish community in Palestine numbered hardly twenty-five thousand. Petah Tikva, my future birthplace, had been decimated by malaria, and the survivors deserted it. That summer, the pogroms following the assassination of Alexander II, started the historic immigration of the Jews to America. It sounds unbelievable, but an appeal to the immigrants to change course appeared that same July in a Jerusalem paper, *Ha'havazelet:*

> What is America to you! Among whom are you going to live! They too are like those whom you are leaving now . . .

> And do not fear the Arabs either, for they are not wild beasts—and we may hope for more from them than from those who are the glory of man and call themselves educated and enlightened.

This letter is extremely funny, but looking at it again from where we stand today, 107 years later, can we even imagine any Jewish present, any Jewish future, without the impact of Israel's being there?

The letter is mad because Palestine of July 1881 had nothing to offer. It was only in September that Eliezer Ben Yehuda would start his one-man crusade for the revival of Hebrew as a spoken language. It would take one more year for the First Aliyah to come into being, and twenty-three years for the Second Aliyah to arrive and have among its few thousands great modern Hebrew writers like Brenner and Agnon.

Here, however, let me quote a few lines from the autobiography *Shanah Rishonah* (First Year) by Shlomo Zemach, who in years to come would leave his mark as critic and editor. In 1904, at the age of eighteen, like his boyhood friend David Ben Gurion, young Zemach left Poland to become a Chalutz. Zemach was brought up as a devout Hasid. During the last night of his voyage to Jaffa, which he spent standing on the deck—so Zemach writes—he felt:

> great sweetness swept me like when I put on my *tefillin* for the very first time . . .

> I narrowed my eyes the way I used to prepare myself during prayer until my temples were in pain and I went on rocking forward and backward, concentrating and aiming my words at the hidden coast-line, at the East: "To Eretz Israel . . . New Society . . . To Eretz Israel . . . New Society.

The moving thing about that prayer is that Zemach was chanting a line from a contemporary Hebrew story, Feierberg's *Le'an* (Whither?), published in 1899, the year its young author died at twenty-five. That scene signifies the role Hebrew literature played in the minds of young dreamers who considered Jewish life in Europe doomed and had undertaken to secure a Jewish future for their people. Zemach was saying his prayers, as "future imagined" was touching the sands of Jaffa, where life was to be realized by the book.

There are many more examples of this repeating pattern, but this is the moment to make a long leap to 1931. Why 1931? Fifty years passed since Jerusalem had asked the immigrating Russian Jews: "What is America to you!" That half-century in terms of Jewish preference itself, was a dismal failure for the Zionist idea, despite the Balfour Declaration. The millions went to America, the thousands to Palestine. By 1931, the American Jewish community had reached the 5 million mark, while in Palestine, with four Aliyot and unceasing propaganda and educational efforts, it hardly reached a miserable 175,000.

And yet, the nucleus of a distinct Jewish society had crystallized by 1931. There was the rich network of political, economic, and social autonomous organizations. But of greatest meaning was that by then Hebrew had become the language of education, from kindergarten to university, of publishing enterprises and public libraries annually enriched with numerous translations from the best of world literature, of public life, administration, the daily press, the theater, and to a growing extent—the home.

Nineteen thirty-one is a memorable year to me personally: I was five and mastered the secret art of reading. At that ripe age I was past kindergarten, student of the Talmud Torah, in which my father was then teacher. My parents were newcomers, hardly six years in the country, but in Poland my father had been teaching Hebrew, while Polish he learned in the army. To me and to all other children around, Hebrew was the only language we spoke, and our Jewish little town—by then a social and cultural mosaic of 15,000 or more—the only environment we knew. To us, that was the world—Jewish, Hebrew speaking. As a matter of course, there were the newcomers and the old, using Jewish languages—Yiddish, Ladino, Jewish dialects of Yemenite Arabic, a substantial group of Bukhara Jews, quite a few Americans, more and more German-speaking refugees—but to speak any of them was unthinkable among us, little kids of the early thirties.

My own home was moderately Orthodox and up to sixth grade I attended Orthodox schools. But at the same time my father encouraged my using the public library, which started my obsession. At that tender age I read abridged Hebrew versions of *Uncle Tom's Cabin, Oliver Twist, Tom Sawyer,* Grimm Brothers, Andersen. As I grew up, I read everything, from Fenimore Cooper to John Steinbeck, from Gogol to Gorky and from Stendahl to Romain Roland, from Goethe's *Werther* to Thomas Mann's *Tonio Kroger* (which I received for my Bar Mitzvah) in the only language I knew, Hebrew.

True, young people like myself accepted the totality of Hebrew in our lives as the most natural thing in the world. The Jew-Goy tension, which to this day plays such a central role in Jewish writing, was simply nonexistent. The mythical Goy was present in our parents' stories and in books, as real as the Gothic World of the Grimm Brothers. As for "those Galut Jews," we were educated to regard them as the negatives of our own self-sacrificing, hard-living, poor parents. The Galut Jews, however, were at the same time our own grandfathers, grandmothers, aunts, uncles, first cousins, always present in the minds of my parents, hardly fourteen years away from Poland when Hitler invaded it. My imagination carved them out of my father's ambivalent stories and my mother's tears. My Hebraist father had never looked back to Poland, while my mother, to her last day—after having lived in Petach Tikva for fifty-five years—had never left her Polish hometown, had never arrived.

Having said that, what do I mean when I define myself as "Jew" and "Jewish Writer"?

Almost half a century after the mythological birth of a generation of de-Judaified "New Hebrews" had been announced in a "Proclamation to the Hebrew Youth" by Yonathan Ratosh, founding father of the Canaanite movement, I wish to state here in plain English, translated from Hebrew:

> I am a Jew, period. My being as deep-rooted in Israel as I believe I am, has always meant to me—and in a profoundly religious way—one thing only: to be an Israeli is to actually embrace Jewishness and stake all future on it. I know, the "in" thing to say would have been, "I am *me, period*," or "I am an *Israeli* writing in my native tongue, Hebrew, period."

Well, I am not, at least not since the summer of 1945 in Europe. It was there, at the meeting of our Jewish Brigade from Palestine with the few who had survived Hitler, that I made up my mind: Israeli (we used to say *Eretz Yisraeli*) means either Jewish, or it is both utterly meaningless and immoral. To me, to say "Israeli, period," is to join those whose inner wish is to escape their Jewishness, to "cease to be." Let us not shut our eyes: Zionism itself is a manifestation of both the "will to be" and self-negation, "the will to become somebody else," to normalize, that is to un-Jew ourselves. In any event, every since that summer of 1945, I consider myself a Jew, period.

And in that, I simply turned my back to myth and embraced the reality of the Yishuv. In reality it was a mishmash of the old Yishuv and of virtual newcomers, of the devout and the secular, of East and West, of Zionists and of refugees exiled to that strip of oriental half-desert. In reality there was very little of that New Hebrew who was supposed to have emerged out of the sea-sands, a breed apart from the Diaspora Jew.

What was reality? One hundred seventy-five thousand Jews in

the Palestine of 1931, most of whom hardly ten years in the country. In a matter of sixteen more years, between 1931 and 1947 the Yishuv grew to six hundred thirty thousand. These figures present us with the actual reality of the Yishuv.

The day Israel became independent, only *one out of every twelve Jewish citizens was either native-born or had been living there for at least thirty years.* All the rest were relative newcomers, *most of them fifteen years or less in the country, every sixth or seventh of them seven years or less.*

The same applies to all the elites of those days. Nothing illustrates the fictitious nature of the myth better than the realities about "The 35,"—who have all fallen in battle on their way to besieged Gush Etzion, the handful of settlements in the Judean hills. "The 35," immortalized in Hayim Gouri's poem *Henay M'utalot Gufoteinu* (Here Our Bodies Lie), have become the metaphorical essence of the Palmach Generation. Who were the thirty-five in reality? A platoon improvised last minute, composed of men from Haganah units in Jerusalem, most of them students of the Hebrew University. Recently, I reread the book published forty years ago to commemorate "The 35," some of the finest of that generation. Fifteen of them, including their legendary commander, Danny Mass, were foreign-born. Danny Mass was twenty-four and hardly fourteen years in the country.

That was the reality, mostly a past invented and a future imagined, but hardly any present at all to rest one's feet on. The most radical example is that of the poet Yonathan Ratosh, born Uriel Halperin. In 1943, Ratosh published his ideological brochure, "Proclamation to the Hebrew Youth," in which we, native-born Palestinian Jews, were declared New Hebrews, a nation apart from Diaspora Jews. I mention Ratosh only in connection with my own view of who Israelis like myself really are. On a personal level, let me just mention the fact that in the late 1950s I worked for the same daily newspaper with this highly original poet, he as proofreader, I as night editor. By then I was already after my experience as a soldier with the Jewish Brigade in the Europe of 1945, after my studies at the university, a self-proclaimed Jew who loved Yiddish as well as a whole-hearted member of the then Zionist Left, and yet Ratosh—refusing to have the word *Jew* written in his ID—was very friendly to me. For one reason only, I knew, I was native-born, potentially—Ratosh never despaired—his man.

I was not, ever.

Fortunately for me, I have recently uncovered in an old literary biweekly the text of what I said in 1954, when my novel *Each Had*

*Six Wings* was awarded a literary prize. This is how that twenty-eight-year-old Israeli of the so-called Palmach Generation described his identification with the then newcomers, the subject his novel:

> The story was not only of those strange-looking newcomers—it was my own story, things remembered from my own childhood, from when my own parents' home was that of newcomers, the story of my own generation, seemingly worlds apart from the so-called "Second Israel" . . .

> [in writing it I also] made use of the folk-songs, proverbs, tales and jokes, the treasures with which I had come across during my studies. That encounter turned into a source of pride and love.

It was a young Israeli's inner conviction in 1954, not at all different from how I view myself today as Jew and as Jewish writer. The miracle makers who had been promising to transport us out of Jewish history and into Israeli mythology had by then stopped to impress me.

Recently I read the letter that old, dying Yekhiel Halperin, Ratosh's father, one of the founders of the Hebrew School in Odessa and Warsaw and a leading educator in Eretz Israel, addressed on 10 January 1941 to his newly born grandson Chaman (who was named after the Pagan Sun-God, and was to be killed forty-four years later in Ras Burka, in the Sinai, by a crazed Egyptian soldier). It reads like the last cry of the dying old Hebrew teacher to his son to free himself from imagined mythologies and accept his own pedigree and his people's real culture. Let me read just the opening lines:

> To my first grandson, tenth generation to the Genius of Minsk, author of "Sequence of the Generations," the memory of the righteous be blessed, may the blessing of your forefathers, Rabbis of Genius, ecstatic Hasidim and scholars at the Yeshivot, authors of profound and penetrating books—rest on your head, my new child. And may you grow to become great in the Torah, in learning and in science, become our pride and glory, an important link in the age-old line of Rabbis and scholars.

Father Halperin's revealing letter strengthened retroactively my position as a stubborn Jew and Zionist. Now I am denied this identity again, this time from the Left. In a piece published as a "New Year Message" in the weekly *Ha'Ir*, Anton Shammas wrote:

Why does the Left in Israel insist on being Zionist, and does not realize that this cannot be—you are either Zionist or Left.

Ratosh, for whom even the Movement for Greater Israel was too minimalist, took leave of Jews, God, and all Zionists, out of an ultranationalist point of view. For Shammas, from a radically different stand, as a supporter of a PLO independent Palestine across the Green Line, the Law of Return is a Racist Law (as he wrote in the 12 October issue of the Israeli weekly *Koteret Roshit*). I cannot be *Left* unless I renounce my racist Zionist convictions. Bluntly put, Israel's Declaration of Independence, which is founded on the concept of Israel as a Jewish State, is a racist document.

What a strange meeting of minds between ultra-expansionist Ratosh and Israeli-Palestinian Hebrew writer Anton Shammas. Territorial Israeliness makes strange bedfellows these days, Ratosh on the Right, Shammas on the Left. I, for one, refuse to imagine myself as if I had a stone for a mother, neither "as a glass or an apple," a freak of nature. Ever since that summer of 1945 in Europe, I consider myself Jew, hence Zionist, hence Israeli, in this order. To me, being Jewish is anything but a disembodied abstraction. It is not only to have had the good fortune to be born at this time and place. It is to have changed from Israeli as an accidental condition to historical Jew as an act of choice.

It is to have lived through this metamorphosis from a state of Jews living in books as territory to living in the Jewish State dreamt up by books; from past-oriented doomed communities to an independent, future-oriented society. It is to have begun life in a tiny immigrant Yishuv, mostly myth, and to have lived to see it as the most vital Jewish community, with a lot of present, an Israel that now actually has a Sabra majority as a massive reality: Two out of every five Israeli Jews are native-born, with a dramatic difference between the old and the young. And Israel of the present day is *young*—54 out of every 100 are under 30. *Nine out of ten of the under-30s*—1,700,000—*are native-born,* and of these, *700,000 have native-born fathers.* This last figure is larger than the entire Yishuv of May 1948.

To an Israeli turned Jew like myself, these figures are the one reality that the affirmative Jew can take comfort from at the end of this century of Jewish solitude and be overcome by a sense of being involved in a mystery. What is it that we have been undergoing? Again and again I find myself going back to Herzl's first entry in his Zionist Diary, which hasn't yet lost its point. What is the essence of this wild Jewish adventure, Israel? Is it a fantasy realized, a state created by the book, or is the book its ultimate realization, as it had happened, more than once, in the past? To be a Jewish writer in Israel, is to be up there on the tightrope, between the two options. We are still in the middle of that invented story, Israel.

# The Story of Creation

## Meir Shalev

A few days ago I met a publisher in New York. Instead of doing business together, we found ourselves discussing another subject—why Jacob wept at the well when he met Rachel for the first time. That's what happens to you after reading the Bible too much. I feel a little awkward trying to speak about the Bible in English, to replace this magnificent rocklike word *Bereisheet,* by "In the beginning," but I can comfort myself with one of my father's tales: when he was serving during World War II in the British army, he was once accompanying a British caravan of trucks from Haifa to Alexandria, it was a long drive and he was talking to the driver of the truck, a British sergeant, a very religious Christian. They talked about the Bible stories and this Englishman was amazed by my father's vast knowledge of the Bible, and he said, "It never occurred to me that they translated this book into Hebrew as well."

When I was five years old, my father, this very father, took me to the valley of Ellah, together we picked five pebbles from the riverbed and read the story of David and Goliath. Since then I became an addict. Since then I believe David was a short kid who wore thick glasses, and I started to suspect that my grandmother was a Moabite woman, though she tried to hide it the best she could.

In Israel, many people believe the Bible belongs to the religious parties. I am a secular person, but the Bible never stopped to intrigue me, influence me, provoke me, and make me envious. It is an old book, written in the precritics period, and is not ashamed to tell us stories about the true, basic, fleshy things of life. The Bible will not tell us about "one afternoon in the life of a poet," nor will it deal with the last night in the life of Otto Weininger, with all due respect. Rather it will tell us about family relationships, hardships of war, love, passion, hate, belief, death—things even intellectuals experience from time to time.

And then, the Bible uses correctly the idea of "literal imagination." That is, provoking the imagination of the reader—rather than boasting his own. The biblical writer will never lift the curtain all the way up. No one knows why Jacob did weep when he met Rachel. Why did Amnon hate Tamar more than he had loved her before, who was the "little girl from Eretz Yisrael" in the Book of Kings, why did Samson reveal his secret to Delilah, and why did man eat the forbidden fruit. This technique made the Bible an eternal cluster bomb keeping to explode ever since.

I would like to discuss here some points in the story of creation. An evasive story no one can fully grasp. Strangely enough, this old mythology is still doing fine today. Darwin did his best to destroy it—and yet it is influential and live. We still use its treasure of ideas and symbols.

In the first chapter of Genesis, we read about God, separating the heavens from the earth, bringing forth vegetation, animals, and sea monsters, setting the two great lights in the skies. At the end of each day, He examined His accomplishments and saw *"it was good."* On the sixth day, when everything was ready, God created the first human couple. Tired but satisfied, he retired for a well-deserved Shabbat rest.

But now the Bible surprises us with a second version of creation. In chapter 2, "God formed man of dust from the ground," *before* any other creature. He sets him down in the Garden of Eden "to till it and keep it."

Many interpreters have pointed out that the Book of Genesis actually gives us two stories of creation with significant differences between them. The religious interpretation of the Bible cannot accept such a point of view, because the two stories present not only two versions, but two distinct types of gods, different in character, aims, and manner of operation. And this is a no-no in a book that boasts the invention of monotheism.

The creator in Genesis 1 does his work by utterance, in remote-control manner, keeping his distance all the while. "Let there be light!" He says—"and there was light." God creates the world, step by step, like some superefficient engineer, checking his work after each step to make sure that "it was good." There are no mistakes. Each piece is fitting into the next, and as the last piece—man—is set into place, God can finally say: "it was very good." A perfect engineering job. Not a single error.

The other creator, in Genesis 2, uses an entirely different set of methods. This God is an artist. He is a sculptor, he is a writer, creating an imaginary place and its characters. He shapes man with his own two hands in a playful, artistic manner.

Maybe that's why, like many other art pieces, it lacks perfection. This is self-evident. After He makes man and puts him in the Garden of Eden, God provides us, Himself, with the key to understanding his creation. "It is *not good* that the man should be alone," He says. This is unbelievable. God, for the first and last time, admits he made a mistake. The expression "not good" is striking when one considers the six times *"it was good"* was repeated by the first God in chapter 1.

Even now, God does not know how to solve the problem of Adam's loneliness. He works according to intuition. He creates the animals, hoping that one of them will please the man, and again, He fails. Adam gives names to the animals, but doesn't find a friend among them. Only then God realizes he made another mistake and he has to approach the problem from a different angle. He takes the rib from Adam's side and creates woman. In the Talmud it is said that "Adam cohabited with each beast and animal but he didn't cool off until he cohabited with Eve." We'll never know if Adam really acted out all the sexual fantasies of the sages, but there is no doubt that both God and Adam tried the "Hit-and-Miss" approach. The Bible says that man was created in the image of God. I think man and God were created in the image of their writers. In chapter 1 the world and the story are a structure of "Lego" stones, very easy to understand. But the creation in chapter 2 is much more intriguing and complex. Here, Man was created alone, and when he opened his eyes for the first time he saw no trees, no woman, no animals. His first sensation, I imagine, was seeing his Creator and feeling his touch. It resembles beautifully the process of "imprinting," described by Conrad Lorenz, the ethologist, in his research of animal's behavior.

The complex character of this God and Adam continues to manifest itself in the episode of the Tree of Knowledge. The tree of knowledge promised the gift of moral judgment to those who tasted its fruit, the ability to distinguish between good and evil. God's injunction against eating it, is in fact, the embodiment of divine will and organized religion to perpetuate man's moral dependence. It is, indeed, the basis of all religious systems. Such a story is not possible in chapter 1, where God and man are not interested in the Tree of Knowledge, but in the tree of know-how. Indeed, in the story of the forbidden fruit, there are two losers—Adam and God, and two winners—the snake and the Chief Rabbinate.

God's failure is double. First He showed his fear from the human threat, just as he did later in the story of the Tower of Babel. But the real irony of the story is that eating the forbidden fruit did not bring about the anticipated results. On the one hand, man did not die—as God threatened he would. On the other, neither did he learn to distinguish between good and evil. As a matter of fact, he learned only one moral lesson: that "good" means obeying God's orders and "bad"—disobeying them.

Adam arrived into the world after his short period in the Garden of Eden. He was burdened by the sweet memory of that garden, and by feelings of guilt and failure.

From the vantage point of organized religion, the God of chapter 2 turns out to have been even more calculating. Guilt, failure, and deprivation are the most effective means for creating a man anxious to satisfy his creator's wishes, without knowing "Which will prosper, this or that, or whether both alike will be good," as in the words of the Preacher.

And so, out of fear and ignorance, systems of religion were born to tell us how and what to do, all of them based on the profound conviction that they expressed the will of God.

Today, most men and women are sure that they are God's most excellent specimens and that their success is a sign of God's grace. They find justification in the fact that they have been created in God's image and are fulfilling the orders of Genesis 1. This is man—king of the beasts and all creeping things (including those who appear to him as creeping things). Even if we aren't exactly biological descendants of this first man, we must have a family connection with the one who wrote the first chapter.

Yet Adam is also there, hiding somewhere inside us. He knows that no material success and no military triumph will bring back his happiness.

This duality reflects the face of Israeli society today. Power, domination, and possessiveness reside side by side with pain and doubt. We are a society of "the chosen people" supported by the God of Genesis 1, and we shout "God is with us!" as so many other societies have done throughout human history. At the same time, we have not stopped to eat the fruit of knowledge for the last 4,000 years. This, I dare say, is our destiny, the Jewish destiny. Like Adam, we know that we, too, are not perfect. We also know that God is not perfect—it's written in the Bible, but this is not something I should say aloud.

# Text, Language, and the Hope of Redemption

## Nessa Rapoport

As a Jewish writer, I am not of the minimalist school of fiction. I am most interested in the possibilities of a literature whose spine and sinews would be not simply Jewish experience but Jewish materials and Jewish dreams.

There have been many novels that evocatively transcribe American Jewish life, but their sensibility has been determined by the Western literary tradition rather than the Jewish one. I want to suggest that just as Western literature is a body of work with a history, from Greek myth to Beowulf and on, so is Jewish literature a body of work—the passionate conversation that took place among centuries of sacred books and their creators, the talking on the page that resulted in law, myth, parable, argument, and ode. As English bears the press of Christianity, so Hebrew carries within itself the books that have forged us as a people—the Bible and the thousands of commentaries begotten from it. And as Western writers are influenced by the body of work that preceded them, and feel able to draw on it—and at times appropriate it—so can Jewish writers retrieve the materials of the Jewish literary tradition for art.

The Jewish novel has been a book for Jews, about Jews, or even against Jews. But the Jewish novel could also resonate with Jewish language and draw its structure, its mode of thought, its allusions from the Jewish books that came before it. Those books were not fiction as we make it today. But they were imaginative readings of sacred texts, and I see the Jewish novel as a descendant of that tradition.

By this I do not mean that a Jewish writer of fiction would replicate the forms of those materials by composing midrash or commentary but that the text of the novel be informed by those earlier texts, respond to them in syntax, diction, and image, immerse itself

not only in the great works of Western culture but in the mostly
unknown body of Jewish writing.

Naturally, if the tradition remains unknown, the writer cannot
avail him- or herself of it. The acclaimed American Jewish male
writers had the immigrant experience to draw on and quarrel with.
They had the music of Yiddish in their ears. They had a tangible
neighborhood anti-Semitism to sharpen their mordant wit. Their
novels taught a generation of Jews to understand itself—torn between the world of European parents and the wild, seductive promise of America, with its non-Jewish women and its non-neurotic
men. It was not possible for those parents to transmit an intimacy
with Jewish texts in the *heder* their children endured, longing for
baseball.

With some exceptions, this was not the experience of my generation, and yet the short stories we read in Jewish communal magazines were often written in a Yiddish intonation derived not from
authentic experience but from imitating the tone of earlier fiction.
They were frequently about the same extremes, the encounter between the circumscribed, nostalgic world of the ultra-Orthodox
community and the postsixties anarchy of secular America. Or
they contrasted suburban Jewish life of the synagogue and the
country club with an idealized portrait of Israel in which everyone
seemed to live on kibbutz.

As any reader, we looked for books that spoke to us, that offered
a vision of Jews or Jewish life corresponding in knowledge and
intensity to the study and experience our parents had insisted
upon: the strong Jewish education at the day schools they established when we were young; the music of Hebrew rather than Yiddish, *modeh ani lifanekha* or *avadim hayinu* or *bishofar gadol
yitakah*—those phrases inscribed on the unconscious by life in
the community, echoes of prayer repeated each day or year since
childhood; and the passion for Israel, not as icon but as knowledge
in the bone, after years of travel and weeks of talk inflected with
street-slang Hebrew.

In vain we looked for ourselves, the invisible Jews who didn't
leave Judaism for a universal truth and didn't retreat to a fundamen-
talist security. What about the rest of us? we wondered, young
Jewish women who could read each month in *Ms.* magazine, many
of whose editors were Jewish, stories about the tribal rituals of
African-American or Chicana women but nothing about the mystery of Jewish ceremonial life. Why weren't our texts, our experience valuable, we wondered, to the overwhelmingly Jewish

editorial boards, anthologists, and teachers directing the next generation of American writers?

We are a people literally saved by a book—and all the subsequent books from it. For centuries Jews have been reading, writing, and honoring words as the manifestation of their immortality. To be a Jewish writer should seem the most august of occupations. Nevertheless, we are still producing mostly doctors. And yet the Jewish writer who has refined his or her imagination on the books that formed us as a people can also heal, by claiming this inheritance proudly and continuing to interpret it; by drawing on the past without enshrining it in nostalgia or proscription; by embracing what is best in American culture only to transform it.

Our texts in Hebrew, Aramaic, Yiddish, and Ladino are not artifacts of an extinct past. They make demands; they offer a vision of a time not like this time. They do not separate the word from the life, asking us instead to take the mundane and hallow it, to release what is sacred beneath the husk of dailiness, to heal the severing between soul and body. The conditions of our life here— the lure of such an unconstrained society, the wealth of many and the temptations of that wealth, the loss of millions who would have taught us what they knew—need a rich body of imaginative work to challenge them.

Of course, my words come from a particular American Jewish context, one that allows me to talk of sacredness and redemption without my being considered—or indeed being—a member of a political party or nationalist movement, as I would be seen in Israel. I want to be emphatic about this: My idea of redemption is not essentially political; it is about the quality of one's soul, and the soul of one's people, and indeed the soul of all peoples, which by definition cannot be completed, or made perfect, in historic time. What is important is that in America I can speak solely as a private citizen of the imagination. On the other hand, the writer in Israel is far more essential to the culture and political life of his or her fellow citizens than the American Jewish writer can be.

And so no one can be a serious Jewish writer here and not turn east. In America we cannot extend Jewish imagination to its most provocative realms—language and sovereignty. We can create a Jewish culture but not a Jewish government; we will never have public transportation whose front seats bear the sign: *mipnei seivah takum,* quoting from Leviticus to remind us to stand so that we honor the elderly. We can play with English, shape and influence the language to a remarkable degree, but we will never hear on national television that the outcome of a football game or an election is *teiku,* a tie, the Talmudic term that means an unresolved debate whose outcome must await the Messiah.

In Israel these instances are taken for granted, part of the unconscious—not self-conscious—texture of daily life. We feel at home in America, but this is not our homeland. It may have been the promised land to those immigrants whose lives inspired fiction, but our people's texts tell a different story.

For thousands of years our prophets and poets have rebuked us on the page or sung praise. They have offered us *hazon aharit hayamim,* envisioning our being worthy of the end of days. Whose words will engage us now? Not, for the most part, our rabbis', often tangled in politics and fear of losing ground. Nor, for the most part, our scholars, embarked on their own important work of lighting what has come before us. Who will dream with us if not the writer, diverting Messianic impulse to the page.

To be a Jewish writer is to be unembarrassed about fiction's possibilities for spiritual grandeur. To be a Jewish writer is to do what Jews have always done: fashion text and language in the hope of redemption.

# Squeezing History into a Teacup

## Max Apple

All the heat and insight and commotion generated (at this conference) has really made me feel like a very old-fashioned thing, something that used to be called a Yid.

I've heard that the shtetl world is sentimental and sentimentalized, that it's gone and apparently good riddance. I've learned that it's been replaced by the world of politics and culture and cosmopolitanism.

I can't speak for Jerusalem and Tel Aviv—I've only been a tourist there and without the Hebrew language—but I've been in New York for a year and a half and on the Upper West Side where I live, I know a shtetl when I see one. The rhythms of that neighborhood, the pulse of its life is Jewish. There are no goats in the courtyards and no thatched roofs but that's merely due to technology and hygiene. I see yeshiva bochers from Columbia and JTS, I notice exotic fruits in the Korean markets when it's *she-hechiyanu* time. My favorite beggar asks me, "Do I say *Gut Shabbos* or *Gut Vach?*"

I'm proud of my cosmopolitan colleagues both Israeli and American for their understanding of politics and culture and its complex relation to our humble business: storytelling and daydreaming. As for me, as a writer, I've never run across an idea I could use. Ideas make my characters so motion sick that they run right out of my stories.

But I do know what Cynthia Ozick meant by substratum. I can't define it either, but in my modern, even better, my post-modern American minimalist avant-garde bones I feel what she called the substratum. I feel it on the Upper West Side and in this room. I've even heard goyim sometimes mention it among themselves. I remember an essay in which C. S. Lewis bitterly attacked T. S. Eliot (even as I say their names I recognize how I love these high-class initials). C. S. was criticizing T. S. for saying that only poets understand poetry and he ended his long argument by concluding that for all their vivid disagreements, the two of them had something much more important than poetry in common, they had the church.

Well, two cheers for them I thought, then and now. What Jew would give up an argument for a shul? We create shuls and varieties of religion just to foster argument.

And as for the question of marginality, no doubt Irving Howe is right, Jewish American literature may be running out of material. But that East European heritage has left us more than ritual—it left us a powerful form of comic irony, that is in no danger of running out soon. In fact, it even works when we take a crack at the world of the Gentiles.

There I see us making lots of progress. Our people never used to be at the pinnacle of Wall Street. There were only Jewish lawyers, now there are lots of Jewish criminals and financial wheeler dealers. And one of these days, maybe even next year, there will be a Jew in the White House. I've read that there might be a seder going on in the presidential dining room. It will be just my luck to miss it. By then I'll be so cosmopolitan that I'll no doubt be spending every Pesach at the Panama Canal or maybe, if we really want to talk about the future, in Russia where Jewish life, even as we speak here, may be unfurling itself in ways that will make American experience seem pale.

On such an occasion, I wish I was a social scientist, so that I could use that terrific word *project* to accurately gauge the future of Jewish American fiction. I might even have a formula—something like the number of best sellers written by Jewish authors, divided by the square of Jewish Nobel Prize winners, then multiplied by the number of Jewish book buyers and adjusted, finally, for lack of Jewish identity, concerns, and knowledge on the part of the readers and the writers.

But even if there was a formula, in this strange business there would still be problems, some just technical, the production bottlenecks of this literature trade—a character waiting years for a plot or the other way around, a story forgotten before it's finished—then add in the Jewish questions and "What is a Jewish novel" becomes about as complicated as "Who is a Jew." And while all this is going on, the writer sits there worrying because he or she knows that time is money, and even worse, it's still time.

It's enough to drive a writer to another kind of work as it often does and would have in my case if I hadn't been hooked at a young age by that stalest of clichés, a storytelling grandmother.

I had no choice. When I got interested in stories I was too young to attend any creative writing seminars. So I stayed home and listened to Bubbe Meises for noncredit.

In our city and especially in our neighborhood there weren't many Jews but I knew that there were a lot of Jews in the important cities. If you had asked me when I was five or six what the most important city in the world was, I'd have told you in a second—Serai, my grandma's shtctl.

I knew more Jews there than I did in our city, Grand Rapids, Michigan, and I liked them. I liked the Gentiles too—those honest peasants who removed their shoes after church to save on the leather and then popped barefoot into my grandma's little saloon to talk about Jesus and have a drink and a bite of herring.

I knew what it was like to sell a wagonload of bread at an outdoor fair and what kinds of problems you took to the rabbi. And long before I understood a thing about love or sex I shed tears for virgins as my grandma gave me the sales pitch her mother used to collect dowries for orphaned brides. Her shtetl became the capital of my imagination, even the setting of my first novel, an unpublished narrative featuring an American Indian transplanted to Serai.

But as I was gathering an introduction to fictional techniques and a sweet history of my ancestors I was also living in the midst of a lower-class and non-Jewish world.

In the good old days before drugs a lot of Michigan boys stole hubcaps and occasionally a car. Veterans of reform school regularly stopped at our house. My buddies in their Elvis haircuts, their jeans low on their hips, swaggered around looking for a fight. They got one if they ever rolled a cigarette out of a T-shirt sleeve on Friday night or Saturday. My grandfather policed Shabbos. Outside they could dismantle parked cars, inside they couldn't light a match. My grampa's fierce Yiddish curses, which none of my friends understood, made them ashamed of their tattoos. My family worried that I might turn out like my friends, but I had no interest in cars. Instead I went to college.

There I studied literature and left my trade-school buddies forever. Always a sucker for a story, I had an appetizer of Greek and Roman tales followed by Shakespeare, then hard-core English moralism—the great tradition, and finally a modern dessert featuring learned allusions and a little Jew-baiting by Pound and Eliot.

I learned to interpret this literature and to love it. I took high seriousness seriously, but for fun I was reading some of the new writers, Bellow and Malamud and Gold and Roth. There was even Isaac Singer whom I remembered from the brown ink of my grandpa's Sunday *Forward*.

But these were not my literary models, I was going to be a writer in the great tradition. I would slip modestly into my spot among the British realists.

But you know what happened? When I started writing none of my stories turned out the way they were supposed to. I wanted epiphanies, little gems of insight that you could respond to with a silent cluck or a nodless nod. I wanted to create the sort of clean quiet people you'd like to sit next to on a plane. Instead I got scrap dealers, and entrepreneurs, and prize fighters, and bossy vegetarians. I wanted a moral order for the universe and I could barely get grammatical order for a paragraph. I was learning to be a writer but not in the great tradition.

I felt more comfortable in the literary neighborhood of certain nineteenth- and early twentieth-century Russians—Gogol who could create a haughty nose dressed as a bureaucrat and an over-coat far more valuable than a man; Lescov with his miraculous steel flea manufactured by a left-handed craftsman; and above all, Isaac Babel whose Jewish narrator could ride with Cossacks and pin a goose on the end of his sword.

My grandmother didn't know these writers, although she did live in Odessa while Babel was still there. She didn't know any litera-ture, a shtetl female wasn't supposed to busy herself with such matters. Still I got a certain kind of Jewish education from her in addition to a general narrative intuition.

My grandfather gave up on me, I was hopeless rabbinic material, my Hebrew school teachers prayed that I would celebrate my Bar Mitvzah in juvenile home but my grandma taught me things.

She knew Torah from the women's Yiddish Chumash, the *Tzena-U-Re'ena*. There the biblical characters often had domestic in-stincts and everyday problems. We spent a lot of time feeling sorry for them. Together we wondered why Moses who could talk to Pharaoh and had his moments with God still couldn't find a Jew-ish wife.

When I told her the story of Jesus as I learned it in school, she told me the "real" story, that Jesus was a *momzer* killed by Jewish women who threw potatoes and cabbages as he flew above them on a carpet. She brought everything down to a human dimension, she squeezed history into a teacup; I drank it and forever after felt at home among myths.

We conducted our conversations in a colloquial Yiddish that I've never completely distinguished from English—that is not from "regular" English. We identified another kind of English, what we called speakers' English. A speaker was someone who came to our annual synagogue dinner and made people feel good about the United Jewish Appeal (UJA). My grandma thought that maybe someday I'd be a speaker but I've never managed, in talking or writing, to get very elevated. It's lucky for me that regular English, even though it's a lot like Yiddish, is good enough for storytelling.

I think the future of this Yiddish-tipped English is rosy. It may not make you feel good about UJA or teach you anything but it's o.k. at the kinds of things Gogol and Lescov and Babel might have noticed, a walking nose like Senator Quayle or a nuclear weapons industry of left-handed craftsmen making steel fleas. It can even remind us that Jews too can play at the bloody sport of Cossacks.

Of course, I'm not talking high seriousness, I'm just applying a little shtetlvision to a few news items. In big solemn America, it still looks to me like a growth industry.

# Of Polished Mirrors

## Cynthia Ozick

(Does the writer have a particular responsibility to the community? Does the Jewish writer have a particular responsibility to the Jewish community? Are there inherent oppositions between the writer and the community? —A response, of sorts.)

The phrase "Jewish writer," I once wrote, "may be what rhetoricians call an 'oxymoron'—a pointed contradiction in which one arm of the phrase clashes so profoundly with the other as to annihilate it."

The oxymoron is one of the most valuable beasts in the writer's stable. It's the beast that makes possible that other creature, Pegasus, who got into such trouble yesterday. The point about Pegasus—for imaginative writers, for novelists and poets—is that he takes *off,* he leaves the earth behind, he leaves *thesis* back down there on the earth. If you try to load thesis—politics, ideas of citizenship, nationality, minority status, homeland, ideas about your *intent* in choosing a language to write in (if you happen to have such a choice)—if you try to load any of this onto Pegasus's back, you ground him. A writer writes in the language that inspires him; no genuinely imaginative writer believes in language as a *political* act.* A mule is that sort of beast of burden; mules are made to carry that sort of responsibility.

So-called "subversive" writing is mule-carried, not Pegasus-carried. Now sometimes readers, critics, historians will use a work made purely out of feathers-of-Pegasus to make a social point; by then the writer is usually dead, and can't protest. But rarely, very rarely, you will find a writer who will himself take a work written aboard Pegasus and load it, *after the fact,* with a cargo of intent

---

*The children in the cistern, for instance, in Anton Shammas's *Arabesques* are purely the children of Pegasus; *they* aren't concerned with the legitimacy of Zionism as the movement of Jewish national self-determination.

and extrinsic political program. And that's when poor Pegasus gets turned into a mule.

Not that mules, donkeys, asses aren't honorable social animals. It's they who make it into the Bible, not Pegasus. Pegasus flies alone.

A Jew doesn't fly alone. A Jew is not a mind alone, year after year, in a room. The Kotzker Rebbe did not go alone into a room until he had committed the terrible act of snuffing the Sabbath lights. And after that, when he was alone in that room, when he hid out in that room with his wild dreams alone, who was to say madness had not fallen over him? A Jew is most actively a Jew when there is a quorum of other Jews. Jews in community learn and daven together and look to one another's needs, a collective devotion in the service of a Unity. *Un Got is eyner, un vayter keyner,* goes the old song, but to know that the Creator is One and there is none other, one must be a member of a community. To be a deep and true monotheist requires the community of monotheists.

How, then, can the essentially lonely and purposefully separated figure of the contemporary writer even approach the idea of the communal? An old event burns in me. There is great hubris in it, and I hesitate to tell it; if I do tell it, it's to define exactly this: writer's hubris in relation to the community. I once had a telephone call from a man of stupendous vigor who had been hugely active in the battles for Israel's independence, both in war and in community agitation, and had continued his activism in all the perilous turmoil of the years since. He was calling, he explained, to engage me in writing necessary polemical tracts. He threw out the name of a certain X, a celebrated American Jewish tract-writer of a former generation. "If only you would commit yourself to such writing," he urged with all his mammoth force, "you could become as well-known as X." I felt abashed. I bleated weakly that my pen owned its single given voice, that it helplessly hunted up imaginary beings, that it lived far more in the creatures of the mind than in the world's immediacy, that it wasn't looking to be well-known so much as it was simply looking to write stories. He took all this in with absolute scorn. In a flaming spirit he lectured me—and he was right—about all the current dangers the Jewish people find themselves besieged by. Our predicament demands, he said, a polemical pen, a severely self-denying pen, a tract-writing pen. Otherwise, he warned, if you do not commit your daily pen to the daily cause, where will you be, what can happen to you? You will drop indifferently into the earth, lost.

I listened; I felt he was right; my Jewish shame grew deeper and deeper. He had pointed me to the proper guilt of the selfish writer who is turned from the community. But suddenly, cornered in my guilt, degraded by my shame, I had a flash. You will probably call it a flash of overweeningness, and you will not be mistaken. But it was also the gleam of another point of view. "Why," I cried into the telephone, "why do I have to be X? Why can't I be Agnon? Is Agnon indifferent to the Jewish people? And Agnon invents, and imagines, and perversely dreams!"

Now of course only Agnon can be Agnon, just as only Singer can be Singer, just as only Oz and Yehoshua can be Oz and Yehoshua. A mini-Agnon, or a minor Agnon, or a splinter of Agnon, is no Agnon at all. But it may be that the principle holds. Ever since that anguished conversation, at least, it has seemed to me that the principle holds. It may be that Jewish writers, simply by *being* Jewish writers, even if they practice a certain aloneness, are anyhow in relation to the community—though not as people who work through political or organizational urgencies are. A writer alone in a room who is writing to bring out a Sharansky from the Soviet Union, or Jews from Ethiopia, or whose pen is entangled with the pressures on and within the Jewish polity, is overtly serving the community, and serving it with intensity. It is much harder to make a case for a writer alone in a room who is writing a story about a rabbi who falls in love with a dryad, or about a Yiddish poet who can't get his work translated, or about the visit of a Jewish fund-raiser with a toy gun in his pocket to a Hasidic town, or about the deranged and loveless wanderings of a survivor of the camps in Miami at night. These are some of the stories I have written, and I don't really know how they can be justified as "communal responsibility."

And yet there may be a way—Agnon's way. Norman Mailer once wrote—I believe it was in *Harvard Magazine*—that there is nothing more damaging to a good intellect than to waste it on Jewish ideas. That strikes me as an insufficient and cowardly statement. David Tracy, a Catholic theologian, has a different and more distinguished claim: "All genuine writers," he says "always ask theological questions." Now it seems to me that writers are always impersonators, impostors, makers of masks. The imagination is free, and allows writers to become whatever they wish, to think themselves into maleness or femaleness, or stones, or raindrops, or Tibetans, or Frenchmen, or the legs of a mosquito. But a writer can never succeed as an impersonator in art if that writer is an impersonator in life. What I mean by this is that a writer must have some metaphysical understanding of who he or she is: where do I come from?

What forces made me? What is my history? Where do I stand in the history of ideas? To pursue these questions in life is the only way to avoid cowardice in art.

A Jewish writer who isn't a coward can write about any subject on earth—any subject, including any gentile subject. A coward can't write genuinely about anything. Any drop of cowardice, like a tiny virus, like a microscopic bacterium, will finally assail all the veins of a writing mind.

Cowardice, I think, comes naturally to Jews in the Diaspora, even in our resplendent America. Fear of standing apart from the majority is only one aspect. There are various forms of cowardice, after all. Nostalgia is one. Sentimentality, the offspring of nostalgia, is another. Both tell lies about history. So-called universalism, which is the offspring of sentimentality, is still another. Tolstoy wasn't a universalist writer; neither was Chekhov; neither was Dickens; neither was Hawthorne; and so on and so on. "Art," says Isaac Bashevis Singer, "needs to have an address." And that is the single indispensable insight writers need to achieve: you have to know where you live. And only after you know where you live can you know how to live; and only after you more or less figure out how to live, can you begin to begin to write.

I suppose the question concerning community is the biblical Joseph's question—a question Chekhov answered. Chekhov said: "Writers and artists should engage in politics only enough to protect themselves from politics." When Joseph, that ingenious economist and inspired man of politics, was filling the granaries of Egypt to stem the future hunger of both Gentiles and Jews, he was clearly serving the life of the community. And by pursuing good politics, he was also protecting his "dream space," as Bellow once called it, from the consequences of bad politics. But when he was listening to dreams, when he was imagining the significance of all those many dreams, when he was Joseph the explainer of dreams, was he somehow outside the community, beyond the community, apart from the community? Surely then he was engaged in no ordinary communal act. Surely then he was engaged in an isolated moment of the mind. Yet the dream runs right on alongside acts in the world. Often it seems like a distraction from acts in the world.

The dream, however, is no distraction. It is the central human purpose around which all politics flows. But how to prove it? How to prove, for instance, that one sentence in a single story of Agnon's is worth an armada of op-ed pieces? Here is how Agnon begins a story: "Naomi had washed the floor, arranged the furniture, watered the flowers, and wiped the inkwells; and the room was filled with peace. I waited for Naomi to finish all her work, and then I would sit down to do mine. For it was a great work I wanted to do, to write down in a book my thoughts about polished mirrors."

A story about polished mirrors! How can one prove that a story about polished mirrors is somehow not of less worth than an op-ed piece arguing for or against this or that political issue? How can one argue that a story about polished mirrors is as much a service as, say, being a nurse or a neurologist in Hadassah Hospital? It is a difficult, perhaps an impossible, argument, and I don't know how to make it. But I bring my devotion to such a proposition, if only out of a tremulous hope of exculpation; the hope that a polished mirror, itself no more than a bauble, will somehow catch a reflection of Sinai.

# Part II
## Jewish Writing in Context

# Section A
## The American Context

# Marginality Revisited

## Ted Solotaroff

Twenty-five years ago, when American Jewish writing was in its heyday, much of the discussion of its prominence turned upon the issues of marginality. Not the most precise concept, marginality had the implication of standing apart, as the American Jewish writer was perceived to do with respect to both sides of the hyphen. Being an outsider in both the American and Jewish communities, he was enabled to see what more accustomed eyes would miss at a faculty meeting in Oregon or on the screen of a western or in the Jewish dietary laws. Marginality also sometimes referred to the overlap between the two cultures where the postimmigrant writer had grown up and considered himself an expert on its various phenomena, ranging from Trotskyism and Freudianism to the riffs of Benny Goodman, the humor of Lenny Bruce.

As Irving Howe suggests, marginality also conveyed the sense of a waning and an adjustment of the more extreme condition of alienation that had been bred by the Depression, Marxism, and the Holocaust as well as by the anti-Semitism and Jewish chauvinism that the writer experienced growing up in the postimmigrant community of the 1920s and 30s. The progress of assimilation has continued to erode the traces of Jewish mores and ethos. The special angle of vision has blurred, and Jewish identity as a subject with a moral edge has tended generally to decline. This development is particularly marked, as one would expect, in the writers of the present generation—the David Leavitts and Deborah Eisenbergs. On the other hand, an unprecedented development in Jewish life is creating a different kind of marginality. If Jewish leaders like Arthur Hertzberg and writers like Philip Roth are correct, and I think they are onto something very important, the new and increasingly tense margin of Jewish consciousness and conscience lies in the preoccupation with Israel. As Rabbi Hertzberg has observed, Israel is the religion of American Jewry and as Mr. Roth has shown, Israel is a rich subject. Part of its great promise for American as well as Israeli writers is its uncanny replication of the precarious, unstable, hemmed-in, contentious, revered conditions of the Diaspora that have all but disappeared in America, which in turn has become the land of Jewish freedom, security, and normality that Zionism envisioned.

On the other hand, the sense of arrival, achievement, and opportunity that the breakthrough sponsored tended to exaggerate the significance of the marginality. After all, a margin that was broad enough to harbor Robert Warshow (an elegant film critic) and Manny Farber (an intensely demotic one), Stanley Kunitz and Allen Ginsberg, Bernard Malamud and Norman Mailer, Irving Kristol and Paul Goodman was bound to be almost as broad as the mainstream it was supposedly set off from. Moreover, it was evident that for many of these writers to begin with, and for almost all of them as their careers subsequently developed, their American rather than their Jewish interests were much more evident. In the context of their careers the Jewish element was typically refracted through their shared disposition to radicalism and their recoil therefrom: it was not until the mid-1960s that such concerns as the Holocaust and the security of Israel began to compete with antiCommunism as the issue of the hour. Similarly, the working out of a literary influence—of, say, Hemingway or Eliot or Edmund Wilson—created a more evident tension in a given career than did the effort to adapt a discernible heritage of Judaism or even of *Yiddishkeit* to American letters.

Instead, then, of being camped on some fertile bicultural margin, American Jewish writing has come to look more and more like the avant-garde of acculturation. Though the writer liked to think he was manning a risky outpost, he was often destined to find the day that the letter arrived from the National Book Awards or the American Academy of Arts and Letters or the English department at Amherst that he had been all along riding an escalator. The real figures of the margin were the European intellectuals, the Hannah Arendts and Hans Morgenthaus and Erik Eriksons and Max Horkheimers et al., whose power of detachment and perception were like a new sun in our sky.

The margin that American Jewish writers actually occupied was so narrow that it is better thought of as an edge. However diverse they may have been in their points of view, they shared a common situation: they stood at an extraordinary point in Jewish history: the end of the Diaspora mentality that was taking place in America. This disjunction between themselves and all those generations behind them of *shtetl* and ghetto Jews, and of a generation or two at most of partially and insecurely emancipated ones, created a characteristic edginess of identity: a concern with who one was now that being a Jew was no longer a fate, as it had been so recently and completely in Europe, but rather was now more like a fact, and not necessarily the central one, about oneself. Instead of the burdens of the chosen people there were now the exhilarations of a choosing one. Except that the terms could become reversed, since a mind-set of centuries doesn't vanish overnight. Hence the tensions, the sharp shifts of focus, the mood swings that characterized the fiction (the writing that was most at the cutting edge of the change) as one went, say, from the coiled anxiety of *The Victim* to the expansive confidence of Augie March to the bitter wages of the American Dream in *Seize the Day;* or from the American pastoral of *The Natural* to the ghettoized New York of *The Assistant;* or from one story in *Goodbye, Columbus* that deals with the overbearing piety of the old urban neighborhood to another story that rebels against the vacuous secularism of the new suburban life. Nonetheless, the main issue was already becoming clear or at least pressing for expression: as the mentality of pluralism waxed and of *Galuth* (exile) waned, the American Jewish writer recognized that he was less marginally American than marginally Jewish. What then did his passage from home (the title of Isaac Rosenfeld's archetypal novel) signify? What belongings was he taking with him?

Because marginality was an elastic concept in the 1950s and 60s, and because their generational experience was fairly similar and their relations often clannish, diverse figures such as the novelist Saul Bellow, the dramatist Arthur Miller, the poet Delmore Schwartz and the critic Alfred Kazin could be brought under the canopy of American Jewish writing and used to exemplify its fresh, independent, and heightened perspectives. In general, American Jewish writers and intellectuals were seen to be hovering intently between residual feelings of disdain for WASP elitedom ("the scrimmage of appetite," as Delmore Schwartz put it, "behind the hedges of privilege") and new or revived feelings of attachment to the postwar America that was diminishing the WASP hegemony and, to some extent, absorbing it. Their experience as born-again liberals or battle-hardened democratic socialists made them particularly alive to the ideological positions, distinctions, and cultural infiltrations that lay between the extremes of McCarthyism and Stalinism in the new political arena of the cold war. (Their political consensus and role playing as former Communists prompted Harold Rosenberg to refer to them in the late 1950s as "the herd of independent minds.") Similarly, their social background made them sensitive to the emerging society—urban, mobile, pluralist, and mass—that was dislodging the traditional communal, class, regional, ethnic, and religious markers of one's place in it. If political realism, urban savvy, and cultural mobility were now the name of the game, it figured that the keen-eyed products of Jewish skepticism and aspiration would have something pioneering to say about it in books like Saul Bellow's *Adventures of Augie March,* Paul Goodman's novel *The Empire City,* Norman Mailer's *Deer Park,* and Grace Paley's *Little Disturbances of Man,* as well as David Riesman's *Lonely Crowd,* Trilling's *Liberal Imagination,* Daniel Bell's *End of Ideology,* Daniel Patrick Moynihan and Nathan Glazer's *Beyond the Melting Pot,* and Leslie Fiedler's *End to Innocence,* etc.

The other—Jewish—side of the margin that the writer-intellectuals bestrode had something of the same dynamic of healed alienation and changes of heart and mind. The accounts of the bitter strife between immigrant fathers and acculturated sons that marked the literature of the 1940s gave way to a more positive evaluation of the Jewish heritage, often by the very same writers. Similarly, the Yiddish that had been so embarrassing when they were children was now the language of Isaac Bashevis Singer and the host of gifted fiction writers and poets before him who were being translated and anthologized. Their work reinforced the view that American Jewish writing was shaped by traditions of moral concern, erudition, dialectical thinking, and vast reserves of self-irony, the one international currency, to paraphrase Isaac Rosenfeld, that the Jews actually controlled. The margin was also said to sponsor a distinctive style that spurned the fanciness and reticence of the literary café for the position-taking, point-making insistence of the intellectual cafeteria.

All of which made good copy in the pages of *Commentary, Midstream,* and *Partisan Review* and, as literary sociology, was more plausible than most generalizations about groups of writers. There was no question that a breakthrough of sensibility was occurring, that it was changing the cultural climate, that it was enabling Jewish writers to feel they had a place as well as positions, and that their Jewish upbringing was no longer to be discounted.

The fiction of this era was characteristically a fiction of conscience, conscience being the main locus of the edginess, for it was much easier for a Jew to stop observing the High Holy Days than to stop observing and criticizing how he and his fellow Jews were leading their lives in an open society. The permutations of the theme are everywhere evident. Now we can see that Saul Bellow's novel *The Victim,* published in 1947, is a major document in the changing of direction and emphasis of Jewish defensiveness from the source of its representative fiction to the object of it. *The Victim,* with one decisive blow of the imagination, turns the theme of anti-Semitism inside out by focusing on the prejudices and resistances of Asa Leventhal as they come under attack from Kirby Allbee, a fallen WASP and former colleague who claims that Leventhal has heedlessly ruined his life and owes him reparation. Most of Philip Roth's stories in *Goodbye, Columbus* some ten years later are similarly devoted to an aggressive and astute exposure of the moral ghetto of Jewish ethnocentrism cemented by self-righteousness that his young protagonists are struggling to escape from. In Bernard Malamud's stories of this period, and notably in his novel *The Assistant,* the New York of the Depression is transformed into virtually five boroughs of conscience, a hard-pressed twilight zone of good and bad faith.

On the other hand, a novel like *The Deer Park*—or a play like *Death of a Salesman* or much of J. D. Salinger's chronicle of the Glass family—is dressed in diverse American styles, as it were, but feels Jewish because of the particular resonance, in each case, of its social and moral concerns. Indeed, much of the literature of "the breakthrough" brings to mind the classic joke about the *nudge* on the Fifth Avenue bus who can't restrain herself from asking the very proper gentleman in a seat across the aisle if he is maybe Jewish. He tries to ignore her, she persists, and finally he admits he is to shut her up. "That's funny," she says. "You don't look it."

Like the brilliant outcropping of modernism among the Yiddish writers of the 1920s, the literature of the American Jewish edge was fed by the dynamics of acculturation that would soon undermine its viability. A work like Cynthia Ozick's novel *The Pagan Rabbi* or I. B. Singer's *Enemies, A Love Story* feels like it is drawing its intensity from the death pangs of the Diaspora: the moral imagination of the writer reconstituting the ethos of Jewish survivalism even as it is fading from the lives of her or his secure middle-class American readers.

Malamud's subsequent career—Bober, the righteous grocer in *The Assistant,* and Yaakov Bok, the wily victim of the blood libel in *The Fixer,* giving way to the Levins and Dubins of academic life, the Fidelmans and Lessers of the arts—provides a paradigm of sorts of the transition that has marked the careers of writers who were raised, to a greater or lesser degree, as Jews who lived in America but have spent the greater part of their adult lives as American novelists or playwrights, poets or critics who happen to be Jewish. As assimilation continues to practice its diluting and dimming ways, it seems evident that the interesting Jewish bargain or edge in American fiction will be more and more in the keeping of writers like Cynthia Ozick, the late Arthur A. Cohen, and Tova Reich, or younger ones like Nessa Rapoport, Daphne Merkin, and Allegra Goodman, who are anchored in the present-day observant Jewish community and who are drawn to the intense and growing dialogue between Judaism and modernity under the impact of feminism, the sexual revolution and the Holocaust. In other words, what remains of the former margin is likely to present itself in the tensions between spiritual and secular being, much as it does for the Christian writer. I'm referring, of course, to Judaism as a living, complex history and faith rather than as shtick, as in Joseph Heller's *God Knows*.

Meanwhile, a new and fertile and increasingly tense margin of Jewish consciousness and conscience has come into being and has only begun to be explored: that is, the relations of American Jews to Israel. Indeed, as Philip Roth has shown in the brilliant second chapter of *The Counterlife,* Israel is our counterlife.

"In the Diaspora a Jew like you lives securely," Shuki Elchanan, Mr. Roth's Israeli commentator par excellence, remarks to Zuckerman, "while we are living just the kind of imperiled Jewish existence that we came here to replace. . . . We are the excitable, ghettoized, jittery little Jews of the Diaspora, and you the Jews with all the confidence and cultivation that comes of feeling at home where you are."

That is the objective side of the situation, as Mr. Roth sees it. He views the subjective one no less incisively: Israel as the very image of the confused desires of American Jews. Again to quote Elchanan: "Reasonable people with a civilized repugnance for violence and blood, they come on tour from America, and they see the guns and they see the beards, and they take leave of their senses. The beards to remind them of saintly Jewish weakness and the guns to reassure them of heroic Hebrew force . . . and out of them flows every sentimental emotion that wish fulfillment can produce. A regular pudding of emotions. The fantasies about this place make me sick."

The rest of *The Counterlife* pales for me beside the vigor and interest of this chapter called "Judea"—as does, to my mind, the body of recent American Jewish fiction. There is an élan everywhere in the pages of Zuckerman's effort to rescue his brother from the fanatic West Bank settlers. Such is generally the case when a mature writer hits upon a genuinely new subject. This extraordinary twist of the dialectic of Jewish history whereby America has become, in large part, the fulfillment of the Zionist dream of full emancipation from the past and Israel has become, in Elchanan's words, the country where "every Jewish dilemma there ever was is encapsulated"—creates, in effect, a multivalent international subject that awaits its Henry James and Joseph Conrad.

Hugh Nissenson and Mark Helprin, two of the most gifted novelists of the middle generation, began their careers by writing about their experience in Israel. Both have developed into shapers of myth, and I'd love to see what each of them would make of the American-Israeli subject now. But the American writer doesn't have to leave home or the immediate realities to tackle this theme, so strongly does the fate of Israel affect and shape the consciousness of American Jews, so firmly is it lodged at the top of the national community's agenda. Since the Six-Day War the survival of Israel has been the paramount concern of organized Jewish life and probably the paramount source of Jewish identity. Given this pervasive and deeply entrenched mind-set, the remarkable thing about Jonathan Pollard the spy is not that he is an anomalous kook, about whom the less said the better, as Jewish officialdom would have it, but rather that he embodies the crisis of conscience that would beset almost any American Jew who came into possession of information that he or she believed to be vital to preserving Israeli lives and that was being withheld. An embarrassment to say the least to the Jewish community's public relations, Pollard is at the same time the product of its ideology, and to say that he was acting out his bizarre fantasies is to corroborate the force of the "counterlife" that Roth has begun to explore.

Other fiction writers, I believe, will follow his lead. Since the Palestinian uprising and the government's response, Israel has moved even closer as a subject; it looms now not only as the hero of our illusions but as the victim of its own; the face that shone its light upon us now bears a grimace, a scowl, a timeless shrug. To the extent that American Jews are marginal Israelis, we find ourselves connected once again to the Diaspora and to the condition of radical doubt that has produced much of its salient modern fiction, from I. L. Peretz and Isaac Babel to Kafka and Joseph Roth, from I. J. Singer's *Brothers Ashkenazi* and André Schwartz-Bart's *Last of the Just* to E. L. Doctorow's *Book of Daniel* and Cynthia Ozick's *Cannibal Galaxy*. We also find ourselves connected to a country with powers and problems that the Diaspora never dreamed of. A Likud government with a free hand in the West Bank and Gaza for the next four years pretty much insures that both the powers and problems will increase and that American Jews will feel even more implicated. In the overlapping area of consciousness that Israeli and American Jewish writers share, the seeds of a new fiction are waiting to sprout.

# Response to Ted Solotaroff: The End of Marginality in Jewish Literature

## Irving Howe

The notion of marginality, often under the more imposing guise of alienation, became central to the self-understanding of Jewish American writers a few decades ago. A declared alienation was, in part, a way of preserving the psycho-social stance derived from Marxist politics while simultaneously abandoning that politics. It also reflected, in part, a genuine feeling of dislocation, or more exactly, of *uncertain* location, among young writers recently emerging from the immigrant streets but starting to find a place in the American literary milieu.

Among the more prominent of these writers, there was usually a mixed feeling about marginality or alienation. Saul Bellow succeeded, for a time, in writing out of quite contrary impulses and premises, no doubt because he felt the pressures of both. A sense of alienation is powerful in his early fiction, and reaches a tragic fulfillment in his wonderful short novel *Seize the Day*. But by the time he wrote *The Adventures of Augie March* he was already repudiating styles of marginality and declaring himself an enthusiast for the openness and (to use a term favored at the time) the "craziness" of the American experience—which might account for a certain *willed* quality in his work, a *stress* upon energy when energy would be enough. Philip Roth completed the turn from marginality.

For other writers of the time, marginality figured ambiguously. If it lurks behind Bernard Malamud's *The Assistant,* in his best stories he writes as if the immigrant milieu were self-sufficient, encompassing imaginatively and sustaining morally for its ethos of affliction and endurance. And thereby marginality seems to evaporate, as a mere indulgence. Something like this might also be said for earlier writers like Henry Roth and Daniel Fuchs, both firmly planted in the immigrant space. They commanded a locale or better yet, a subject commanded them, and thereby they came into possession of a scale of values that allowed them terms of self-definition. Perhaps the most sensitive perception with regard to marginality appears in the work of Delmore Schwartz, especially in his beautiful story "America, America," where Shenandoah Fish (the very name a comic suggestion of psychic fissure) hopes, probably in vain, to dissociate himself from his own smugness as an intellectual looking down upon the older, immigrant generation.

In the experience, then, of the Jewish American writers marginality serves a number of uses:

These writers had left behind the immigrant world but its stigmata were still stamped on their souls. Nearing high culture but uneasy with its manners and maneuvers, they tried to carve out a little space for themselves, practically and imaginatively. If they were uncertain, however, as to who they were, they knew what they had been. Did not the mere fact of becoming an *American* writer signify a subtle betrayal, though why or of what was unclear. To stay with the old folks, we all felt, would mean provincialism and tedium; a refusal of gifts from Western culture. (Parenthetically, the great Yiddish poet Yaakov Gladstein once said to me, "We taught them how to read, and then they went to T. S. Eliot.") Such embarrassments, overcome after a time, reflected a transitional experience, just as Jewish American writing can itself be seen as a transitional experience.

Marginality was itself part of a tradition, inherited from the immigrant milieu. Rubbing up against an alien culture, the immigrant Jews had first to pull inward in order later to move outward, with collective identity serving as a springboard for individual dispersion. Yet in that interval the immigrant world gave its literary offspring a lovely blessing: it gave them memories, it gave them evocative place names and dubious relatives, it gave them thickness of milieu. Their marginality was thus indistinguishable, for a while, from an overpowering, and even oppressive sense of community. But that's what writers need: the pressure of inescapable situations.

The rhetoric of marginality also served as a strategy for the New York writers, identifiably Jewish yet not identifying themselves as Jews—a strategy by which they could briefly maintain what I'd call their politics after politics; by which they could band together for common ambitions; by which they could give symbolic status to an uneasiness they could not always name.

Perhaps the most important meaning, ultimately, of marginality was as a way to initiate, all but unconsciously, a link with nineteenth-century American writers like Emerson and Thoreau, Whitman and Melville. Despite a professed distaste for the Emersonian tradition, which for many years I foolishly shared, the Jewish American writers were in part reenacting some of the styles and postures of that tradition. The great nineteenth-century American writers had been inspired by a vision of human possibility that, as it faded into helplessness and despair, also became a fierce critique of America society. Most Jewish American writers consciously aligned themselves with the cultural modernism of Europe, though uneasily, since they knew about its deep strains of reaction and even anti-Semitism. Yet I think it can be said in retrospect that American Jewish writing represented a slow coming to terms with American culture, first as a curious repetition of the strategies of American regionalism, in which writers breaking out of provincial settings create themselves as adversaries of a national center that is probably not even present, and second, as a partial and rather awkward inheritor of Emersonianism, not so much of its doctrines as of its adversarial stance. For the Jewish American writers were steadily becoming Americans, Americans above all.

In a fine essay, the Southern writer Eudora Welty discusses the ways in which the physical setting of a story establishes and validates its meanings. Place is where the writer "has his roots, place is where he stands; in his experience out of which he writes it provides the base of reference, in his work the point of view." Far from being mere inert locale, place becomes an organizing principle in the work of fiction. Bellow's Chicago, Henry Roth's East Side, Daniel Fuchs's Brooklyn: to visualize these settings is to grasp theme and idea. As Welty writes: "The moment the place in which the novel (or story) is accepted as true, through it will begin to glow, in a kind of recognizable glory, the feelings and thought that inhabited the novel (or story) in the author's head and animated the whole of his work. . . . Location is the crossroads of circumstance, the proving ground of 'What happened? Who's here? Who's coming' and that is the heart's field."

The heart's field. A lovely phrase. The heart's field for many American Jewish writers will forever be grey, packed streets that they kept in memory long after the actuality was erased.

American Jewish fiction has primarily been a fiction of immigrant life, intimately known and nervously recalled. Delancey Street, Pitkin Avenue, Napoleon Street, these are inducements, props, stimulants. Place, insofar as it becomes "the heart's field," also entails a cluster of inherited styles and values, ways of life—as well as specifically literary styles yoking together mandarin refinements with gutter vividness, inherited demotic with acquired high culture. What this meant for the American Jewish writers was, above all, the advantages, and limitations also, of an inescapable subject, with abundance of memory turned into discipline of narration.

American Jewish fiction, drawing heavily upon the immigrant locale, finds its substance and its value in a Jewishness of experience. The most recent Jewish writers, perhaps as talented and probably more knowing than their elders, lack this resource; for them Jewishness appears as a problem, a sentiment, a commitment. Harold Brodkey in one story has a character say that "being Jewish was a great truth," but what that truth consists of, and how it manifests itself in life, seems very elusive in his writing. This is not a fault, it is a condition. For we are witnessing a transition from *Jewishness as experience* to *Jewishness as essence*. Intellectually, the latter may even be preferable, since the Jewish experience of the earlier American Jewish writer was one in which much of Jewish tradition, learning, and knowledge had been lost. Those who think of, or write about, Jewishness as an essence—a religious or metaphysical content— may indeed be seeking to affirm a stronger connection with the Jewish past. But for literature, for the writing of novels and stories, the experience of the writers who came out of the immigrant milieu provided a richer setting, a more accessible dramatic substance, a more powerful and enclosing subject.

And that is why I am a little skeptical about Ted Solotaroff's prescription, if it is that, at the end of his paper: that writers turn to the relations between American Jews and Israel. For intellectual debate, political analysis, cultural essays: yes. For fiction, it all seems to me too entangled with polemic, too distant from common life. And the example of the Pollard case that he gives strikes me as better for a Graham Greene or a Joseph Conrad than for the younger Jewish American writers. I do not wish to seem dogmatic on this matter; the future may prove me wrong. But my inclination is to believe that while there remain of course many areas of American Jewish life open to scrutiny, from the suburbs to the *makhers* to the universities, they are too diverse, too lacking in dramatic concentration, too unfocused conceptually for ready fictional treatment. There is, in short,—or so I think—*a crisis of subject matter* and it is not likely to be overcome very soon.

But this crisis—which, in the barest shorthand, I designate as the transition from Jewishness as experience to Jewishness as essence—is only secondarily a literary one. It is actually becoming the crisis of nonreligious Jews themselves, who search, with varying degrees of seriousness and authenticity, for some residual—

symbolic, analogical, "cultural"—fragments with which to retain a Jewish identity steadily being drained of substance. No example of this could be more poignant than some recent writings of Harold Bloom, in which he tries to establish, in a sort of inspired madness of analogy, Freud, Kafka, and Scholem as new centers of conviction for secular Jewishness: an effort he himself admits must at best be confined to an elite and that ineluctably cuts itself off from what has traditionally been source and base of Jewish existence, namely, the folk as community of shared belief.

Finally, a few words on the question: Why so much talk about American Jewish writing? In American literature it is a fairly minor phenomenon. There has not been one Jewish writer comparable to the great nineteenth- and twentieth-century gentile American novelists and poets. What we can reckon with is one major novel, *Call It Sleep,* Fuchs's fine trilogy of Jewish life in Depression Brooklyn, some of Schwartz's stories, a few novels by Bellow, etc. Impressive, but hardly warranting the hullabaloo that has occurred. I have a few speculations:

(a) It was all part of Jewish self-consciousness, Jewish self-advertisement, part of the painful struggle of a minority, non-Christian subculture, to establish itself in America. A certain amount of exaggeration was unavoidable.

(b) It was also part of the effort of the *Partisan Review* circle to consolidate its claims to literary importance. If the New Critics had Warren, Jarrell, and Lowell, then the New York critics came back with Schwartz, Bellow, and Malamud. A certain amount of exaggeration was unavoidable.

(c) The interest of the American Jewish community in American Jewish writing (it doesn't by the way extend to Israeli writing) served it in extremely important ways. This helped, or seemed to help, fill the spiritual vacuum that has become increasingly evident—*a glaring emptiness*—at the center of American Jewish life. With the fading immigrant Yiddish culture and the disinclination of most American Jews to take religion seriously, the Jewish community became dimly aware that it needed "something" other than check writing, banquets, and lobbying to justify its claims to cultural substance. Half in submission and half in resentment, it turned to the very Jewish American writers it felt to be excessively "negative." There followed a serio-comic misunderstanding which forms all too large a part of what passes for so-called Jewish American culture.

And then, even this began to slip away. It did not last. It could not.

# Tradition and Renewal

## Alan Mintz

I want to begin with two observations about the origins of modern
Jewish writing in the late eighteenth century; these are perhaps
obvious points, but ones worth underscoring in order to understand how we got to where we are now. The first point is the following: A necessary precondition for the emergence of modern Jewish
literature was *the contraction of the domain of Torah in the experience of the Jew.* Literature qua literature rather than as a hand-
maiden to liturgy or exegesis or popular education, literature as
an institution possessed of its own value and occupying its own
ontological niche—this is something new that comes with the modern age. This autonomy of value is not the same thing as art-for-
art's sake; Jewish literature was often enlisted in the service of
such ulterior motives as social criticism, ideological exhortation,
and existential and even religious pursuits. But literature did claim
its own prerogatives, and these necessarily in their time came at
the expense of, and as a symptom of, the authority of Torah as the
sacred circle of meaning in which the life of the Jew was inscribed.
One needn't resort to the full measure of severity taken by Cynthia
Ozick at times in identifying art with paganism and opposing it to
belief in order to admit to an essential break between writing as
we know it and the Jewish religious tradition. This rupture must
be insisted upon, for in our talk about renewal, which often takes
on a wistful, romantic, and optimistic aura, we lose sight of just
how far our imaginative lives have traveled from the inscribed circle
of Torah.

My second point goes to the issue of Hebrew versus English,
or, put more historically, the relationship between modern Jewish
writing in Jewish languages (primarily Hebrew and Yiddish) and
modern Jewish writing in European languages. My perspective is
a historical one, and I believe I can identify the moment in the late
eighteenth century when Hebrew literature and Jewish literature
in non-Jewish languages set off on divergent courses. I speak of

72

the publication in 1793 of that wonderful book, Solomon Maimon's *Autobiography,* which tells the story of Maimon's origins as a Talmud prodigy in Poland, as an *iluy,* his wanderings in search of enlightenment, and his eventual arrival within the favored circle of Berlin philosophers. Maimon's *Autobiography,* to the best of my knowledge, is the first great modern Jewish story that is written by a Jew in a non-Jewish language, in this case in German. Maimon's example is instructive for our purposes in two ways. First, the choice to write in German was a choice to tell the story in such a way that it would interest, and along the way entertain, gentile readers or Jewish readers distant enough from their origins to appreciate the ethnographic information Maimon was providing. Second, the story Maimon had to tell was a story about a journey outward, a trajectory of escape from the Jewish community, and the story is told, of course, from the position of achieved acculturation.

Beginning with Maimon, then, it was the theme of acculturation—using the term descriptively and not judgementally—that became the preeminent subject of Jewish literature in the West in German, French, and English. Certainly the classics of American Jewish literature are principally concerned with how the individual Jew negotiates the transition from the densely ethnic immigrant milieu into the broader life of American society. This movement is never smooth or linear; it is filled with ambivalence and irony, accelerated by desire, retarded by regret, leavened by humor; but its general direction, a movement outward, is rarely in question.

Let us shift the focus for a moment to a parallel context: the new Hebrew literature that began to be written in Eastern Europe in the nineteenth century and later established itself in Eretz Yisrael. Like its Western counterpart, this literature, too, is concerned with the alienation from origins. If we think of the great modernists at the beginning of the century (Berdichevsky, Gnessin, and Brenner), the break with the tradition described in their works is, if anything, much more violent and painful. In addition to the ambivalent alienation from family and community, there is a cognitive and theological crisis attendant upon the sudden collapse of the world of Torah, and this is a dimension largely absent from American Jewish literature. Yet on balance, both Jewish literatures, East and West, proceed from this point of departure, the rupture with tradition whether in the guise of family culture or religious symbols. The truly consequential difference, I would argue, lies in the choice of language and in the audience that choice brings with it. For the Jewish writer at the turn of the century the decision to write in Hebrew implied many things—the favoring of Hebrew over Yiddish, an identification with the Jewish national movement—but at bottom this meant a choice to communicate with, and *only* with, a Jewish readership.

This may be an obvious point but one that I think is critical to delineating the constraints and options that operate differentially on Israeli literature and American Jewish literature. The Hebrew writer, by virtue of the language he or she has chosen, conducts a dialogue within a *bounded* community of readers. Amos Oz and A. B. Yehoshua, I imagine, are pleased to be published in English and other languages, but when they sit down to write, their interlocutor is a Hebrew reader. (In the case of Aharon Appelfeld as Robert Alter has mentioned, I am not sure this is true.) From its beginnings, Hebrew fiction allowed itself to be unsparing and at times ferocious in its critique of Jewish society. In doing so, it continues the Haskalah tradition of serving as a *tsofeh leveit yisrael,* a "watchman for the House of Israel." This critique can be undertaken because it is, of necessity, within the family. This accounts in part, I think, for the equivocal reception of Israeli writing in America. Novels of considerable artistic merit that are wildly successful in Israel often are not taken up by large numbers of American Jewish readers when they appear here in translation. We are not part of the code or covenant created by Israeli writing in Hebrew. Conversely, how else to explain the Philip Roth syndrome in American Jewish literature whereby the anger of the community is provoked by an unflattering picture of itself, and this reaction and the writer's reaction to this reaction become in turn the stuff of art? If the Roth example is perhaps an extreme one, it nevertheless illustrates the composite and ultimately uncontrollable make-up of the audience for American Jewish writing, and it underscores the set of sensitivities and awarenesses that must inevitably derive from this fact. These are, at least, my presumptions about a fundamental difference between writing in Hebrew and writing in English, and I look forward to hearing from the practitioners of these crafts themselves among us here whether they find this to be true as well.

I wish now to return to the specific subject of our session this afternoon, the question of Jewish tradition and Jewish renewal. Here again the factor of language is key. If we take the issue of tradition at a more generalized level, at a level in which the tradition has an influence in terms of its themes and motifs and the resonance of historical events, then the question of Hebrew versus English is perhaps not so pointed. But if we speak of engaging not the motifs and figures but the texts of the tradition, then the problematic that characterizes the two literatures is in fact quite different. What is difficult and what requires a special programmatic intention in English, turns out in Hebrew to be inescapable, or very nearly so. Let's look first at the case of Hebrew and then of English.

The place to look for the changing relationship to tradition in Hebrew literature is in the development of Hebrew style. The new literature, we've said, was born out of a rebellion against the tradition. It sought to use Hebrew to describe a human space, either collective or individual, that was neither liturgical nor sacred. Yet at the same time no such linguistic instrument existed; the only Hebrew that existed was the Hebrew of the classical texts, and it was out of this material that the task had to be undertaken. The central trope for the emergence of modern literary Hebrew of the past two hundred years is the act of disentanglement, and that process with its many modulations has recently been described with great penetration by Robert Alter in his new book *The Invention of Hebrew Prose.* The style of the *maskilim* in the nineteenth century was essentially a pastiche of biblical phrases; this in turn was transformed by Mendele (Abramowitsch) into a vibrant organism that exploited all the historical levels of Hebrew for the purposes of social satire. This grand style, called the *nosah,* was in turn taken apart by Brenner and Gnessin, who used the materials of the tradition to fashion a language capable of describing the flux of individual consciousness. And so the story proceeds; the point is that for the Hebrew writer Hebrew is necessarily a palimpsest in which the negated or discarded meanings of the past coexist— in however ghostly a fashion—with the chosen and constructed meanings of the present. The Hebrew writer can make active and ironic use of these latent presences or he or she can struggle to keep them out and strive toward a Hebrew that is purified of historical resonance. But it will always be a struggle, because the history of the language, like a river channel continually silting up, will always have to be forcibly displaced.

Now when we turn our attention to American Jewish literature, the case is very different. I can think of several early writers who attempted actively to use Jewish sources in their writing: Henry Roth's heder scenes using Isaiah in *Call It Sleep;* passages in Charles Reznikoff's poetry; and of course the ambitious but largely unrecognized verse of A. M. Klein. However, in the mainstream of American Jewish writing, certainly in the fiction, the elements of Jewish life that are selected for representation are not the texts of the tradition but social and sociolinguistic manners, preeminently the speech of first- and second-generation Jews. And little wonder, given the thin and unraveling texture of Jewish life in America during those years.

In recent years there has been a countermovement in American Jewish writing, a development in which the genuine materials of the Jewish imagination have been drawn upon rather than merely the social reality of the way most Jews live now. The extent and depth of this change is a question we shall need to address: how much of this countermovement is in fact vision, a kind of wishful rhetoric, and how much is a reality? Must literature of necessity be based on an existing social matrix, or can it be produced by ideas, by visions, or by a resort to the text, all of which do not necessarily proceed through the thickly and densely populated reality of a social life?

# What's New in American Jewish Writing

## Rosellen Brown

The writer sitting down at his or her desk does not often think in terms like *culture* and *substratum,* which are analytic words that present themselves, usually to others, after the fact. Theoretical issues lurk, of course, behind every choice, but they are covert, or should be. If anything, their prominence when they assert themselves in questions of duty and obligation—"What issues should I as a 'Jewish writer' be engaging?"—can be destructive and misleading. And of that sense of debt which appears to puddle up from time to time in many writers of what they used to call "Jewish extraction"—an interesting phrase that hints at removal and repair!—comes some terrible writing that clarifies few confusions and gives little authentic pleasure.

I want to draw on a very interesting, if often discouraging experience I embarked on last fall. My husband, Marv Hoffman, and I were invited by *Tikkun* magazine to become the fiction editors for this liberal, engaged journal that calls itself a "Jewish critique of politics, culture, and society." Our editorship means that dozens of manuscripts pass across our desks (though fortunately the staff in Oakland takes care of dispatching most of them). We read unsolicited manuscripts, we write to our friends, to writers whose work we've seen in other magazines and liked—we take all comers— and yet, in spite of the rather astonishing numbers of stories we see, we find very little that passes muster. The difficulty of finding good fiction is always hugely increased by limiting or in any way delineating subject matter or approach: Once I edited an issue of the literary magazine *Ploughshares,* in search of stories written by men from a woman's point of view and vice-versa—an exercise in writing as another, an *other*—and if ordinarily one percent of submissions might have interested me, I think I was reduced to liking about one hundredth of one percent by the imposition of my thematic scheme. But for *Tikkun,* I think, we are looking for a much broader range of work, far broader than most people tend to understand. Well, what do we say we are looking for?

We start by positing that *something* needs to separate a *Tikkun* story from a *New Yorker* or an *Esquire* story—not that they might not want to publish some of what we print—in fact we share a number of writers—but rather that we would not find most of their work particularly relevant to our needs. What does this mean? Virginia Woolf, you may remember, asks at the beginning of *A Room of One's Own* what we mean by "women's fiction." Fiction written by women? About themselves as women? About anything? Or fiction written by anyone about women? The Jewish Book Fair that sells 10,000 books every fall in Houston, where I live, is assaulted, I think, by the same slippery question as it relates to Jewish writing, and they solve it, or at least approach it, by casting as wide and perhaps as undiscriminating a net as possible. Thus books with absolutely no discernibly Jewish content are featured because their author's name is identifiably Jewish. I should add that plenty of people get passed over by such a crude measure: my first novel, *The Autobiography of My Mother,* which raises a great many questions for Jewish readers and features a heroine—perhaps an antiheroine—whose psyche is, I think, profoundly affected by her conception of Jewish history, was never marketed as a "Jewish" book, and since my name is Brown, it was invisible to the people who were out scouting for people named Klein and Schwartz. Some, on the other hand, think they can swim into that wide net by making rather casual adjustments, like the writer who sent a story to *Tikkun* in which he'd crossed out the name of his protagonist, which I think was Neilson, and quite visibly made him Bernstein—circumcised, right before our eyes, by a flick of the pen. We were not so easily deluded.

Because, I think, it reflects the popular understanding of what constitutes "Jewish" subject matter, I want to give you a short list of the most common species of story we receive—or maybe the genus is Jewish fiction and each of these is a species. (I will now probably offend half the audience, who has submitted such stories to us, or to someone.) This is a close-up view of what Irving Howe called "a crisis in subject matter," abetted, as I see it, by a crisis of form as well.

By far the most frequent subject, we have found, is the aging parent or old person, often an immigrant; if not, then someone still in touch with old wisdom impossible to duplicate today. Usually a younger consciousness is represented in the story; he or she (obviously a surrogate for the author) is fairly abject with helplessness and grief at the declining state of the Old One, or with eagerness for moral or religious instruction, presumably before it's too late. These stories are not often deeply engaging; they tend to be dutiful and guilt-struck and they let the character—and perhaps the author—off the hook rather easily, as if to say, well, that's the end of *that,* to go about the business of their secular lives without finding a live and vital source for their Judaism. This is a kind of death rattle Judaism, spasmodic, a short phase. (I have to admit I've perpetrated a few myself: my father-in-law has had plenty of time in my stories, but I've tried to avoid the worst pitfalls of the genre by focusing in fact on a foreground character whose life has its own dramatic trajectory.)

The next most frequent subject attempts to deal with the Holocaust. It's not so much that these earnest stories trivialize the horrors they approach; and in a certain sense it's admirable that our generation, and a still younger one, wants to try to feel some fragment of that pain. It's just that their sheer inadequacy is either deadening or unintentionally *chutzpadich.* The Holocaust is a black star; our little words implode and leave a gaping hole where feeling needs to be. And no surprise. They would do better to leave it alone. (The only interesting story we have found that approaches the subject, by a young writer named Marcie Hershman, turns its eyes slightly to the side and gives us some offstage movement that illuminates beautifully something of the—possible—psychology of a Nazi underling; there are no camps in the story; there is only a modest and subtle study of some of the shadows on the cave wall.)

Next most popular, I'd say, is the memory-of-Brooklyn story, which sometimes takes place in the Bronx: Bar Mitzvah lessons at the hands of a barbaric, or sweet-and-impotent, or grievously-misunderstood-and-underpaid-but-profound old rabbi who usually smells of garlic and whose pants are shiny with wear. Or beatings-in-the-park-at-the-hands-of-goyish-thugs stories, vaguely derivative of Isaac Babel. And so on.

What you can probably see emerging here is a pattern—namely that the majority of these stories document old news. The word for that is nostalgia. What is identifiably Jewish in the lives of the writers lies almost entirely in memory now, a pool not newly replenished because their current lives are not notably heavy in which you might call Jewish content. Nor do they understand that for the purposes of fiction making, they can subject their moral lives to a kind of questioning and accountability that some of us would recognize as specifically, if not exclusively, Jewish. They are reflecting, distantly, and with a certain poignant sense of loss, the disappearing Jewish lives of others, which for them are the only ones in sight. If I want to think Jewishly, these writers seem to be saying, either I remember Bubbe and Zaide, Auschwitz, Reb Mordechai, or the time the O'Brien twins nearly slaughtered me and left me for dead in Crotona Park.

The two obsessions with current life (with which I am not unsympathetic but which are rarely worked out with sufficient complexity) are the I-am-woman-and-I-will-assert-myself-somehow-in-the-patriarchal-tradition story, and the American-in-Israel story, usually—in fact, in my experience, always—fragmentary and inconclusive, the main character torn apart by contradictions and inconsistencies but appreciative nonetheless of the vitality and beauty of the sabras, not to mention disgusted by their—whatever: arrogance, belligerence, sexism, cruelty to Arabs, and so forth. Aside from the larger issues of identity, it is impossible for an American Jewish writer in Israel not to respond to the sheer human texture of the place, the vitality, the color, the rasp and crackle of so much street life, even if he or she could leave aside the hard questions. But perhaps as an act of humility born of limited experience in Israel, our response seems always to be fragmented, provisional, a gathering of random impressions.

Now you might say, mediocre stories are mediocre stories no matter their subject matter. Here I want to raise some writerly questions since, clearly, being "p.c."—politically correct—or "c.c"—culturally correct—does not guarantee that you can make art of your concerns. The stories I was speaking of tend to suffer from a confusion about what, to use the film critic's word, the writer's gaze actually takes in or pauses over. Over-earnestness about searching out relevance and significance tends to make them sociological rather than artful, heavy-handed where they need to be light-footed.

John Hollander speaks most wonderfully about this problem in a recent essay on American Jewish poetry. He quotes Dante, using an apt phrase from *The New Life,* that speaks of "a screen for the truth." (Freud, of course, spoke of "screen memories" in a similar vein.) Dante is referring, Hollander says, to an unnamed lady past whom he was looking, in a church full of people, at his secret muse, Beatrice d'Este. This lady sat in his line of sight, and everyone believed he was looking at her, but of course he has made of the lady "a screen" for his true preoccupation, at whom he could look his fill, but obliquely. For poets, Hollander says, and I add fiction writers with little hesitation, "the result will always be that the subjects of poems are no more what they are 'about' than their verse-forms are." Substitute stories and forms of stories in the sentence.

But many Jewish writers, though they feel obliged to deal with it, are uncomfortable in the presence of so-called Jewish matter: they don't live it much, or think consciously in its terms, and so you can see them taking a deep breath before they plunge in and swim hard to get to the other side of the unfamiliar and perhaps dangerous waters. Paul Celan, speaking for his era, observed that his Judaism was less thematic than spiritual; Kafka said nearly the same thing. The majority of the work we see is thematically hard-breathing and anxious. And where its spirit is I have no idea, except that it seems bent on discharging a long-forgotten obligation.

As a sort of parenthesis, I want to add that I think part of the problem of finding good but subtle stories that will make provocative reading for us lies in the difference between novels and stories. A novel can use the Jewishness of its characters as a background color (by which I don't mean incidental, but rather encompassing), can utilize and exemplify the assumptions that exist in our universe as Jews—historical, circumstantial—without necessarily making them the sole focus or subject. When Jay Neugeborn, for example, writes about Jewish gangsters in *Before My Life Began*, we aren't asked to spend much time saying "What a phenomenon, a Jewish gangster!" Their Jewishness is a given; it is their universe. What do they do within it—that's what interests the author. What are these gangsters' lives like? The sheer length and complexity of a novel militates against simplification. Novels have the amplitude to paint characters into a rich landscape, but landscape, except in Man Against Nature books, is background; stories, on the other hand, tend to search for a single symbol that will contain meaning. Because the story is so compressed, so aimed—too aimed, most of the time—it ends up being, as Hollander said about poems, only what it is about; it is, all in a rush, no more than its subject. In addition, many of these stories keep referring to an offstage life we are presumed to understand because we have shared it: they use Jewish culture as public reference, its challenges and absurdities agreed-on, like an in-joke, a poke in the ribs between familiars. They are, in that sense, intensely parochial and exclusive and haven't much independent life. It seems to me that a good story is amphibian: it can live in its native waters but can also exist comfortably on the shore amidst readers who are not part of the *meshpuchah*.

Anything a Jew thinks can make a Jewish story. Anything anyone thinks on subjects a Jew gives thought to can make a story of interest to Jews, though not perhaps a Jewish story. How one chooses, well or badly, a road to walk; how one knows the Law in its day-to-day manifestation, whether it is called the Law or not. Sometimes these stories will ask their questions in traditional Jewish terms, whether visionary or pragmatic, or restore some historical scene for our imagining, fleshed out like Midrash around a laconic text. The person asking "How shall I live? Am I my brother's keeper? And who is mine?" does not need to be named Shapiro and he need not ask the urgent question before the Western Wall or the open ark or over his open siddur; he needn't ask it in steerage or on 7th Avenue or Maxwell Street. He, or she, will ask the question of history and of himself or herself. And if he or she believes in God, he or she will be heard by God.

We are coming to the end of Yiddish accents and the Evil Eye but we are still a people who share ancestors and geography and a tradition of bold and sometimes—often—heretical questioning. The new grandparents live in Florida and tool around artificial lakes in pedal boats. In another half-generation there will be no more pinochle. But theirs are not the same ancestors who came on the *Mayflower* or, straight from a farm in Norway, settled in Minnesota, or died in slavery, or swam across the Rio Grande. And so I presume we ask our questions in a slightly different tonality. I do believe in what Amos Oz has called "a shared set of sensibilities."

Here is a case in point. My own most recent novel, *Civil Wars,* concerns a couple, old civil rights heroes; it is set in Mississippi fifteen years after that momentous time in American history, and it poses a number of questions: how one is obligated to act toward the stranger in one's midst; the terrible costs of unyielding—self-righteous—commitment even to a good cause; these and many more. The wife in my book is Jewish—a red diaper baby, whose father was an old Communist who went underground during her childhood in pursuit, perhaps excessive, of his ideals. Her husband is not Jewish; but she is for the first time conscious of her Jewishness when her niece and nephew, who come, like a doom, to live with them, turn out not only to be little bigots bred in a segregationist household but also Christian fundamentalists. Now it happens that the civil rights movement was rife with Jews and with the sons and daughters of ministers who took their fathers' sermons seriously. And so, making my character Jewish was historically plausible, even probable. Making her self-conscious about *halakhah,* or observant, or even preoccupied with her nominal religion would have falsified my experience of the 60s.

And yet I see *Civil Wars* as a "Jewish novel" because—simply—
it tries to place a Jew in history. It tries to describe a moment
when the progressive, left-wing, more or less secular background
so common to American Jews intersected with a formative moment
in twentieth-century American life. (Another book comes to mind,
*The Organ Builder,* by Robert Cohen, which concerns itself with
a young man named Heshie Friedman, whose father, a physicist,
was part of the Los Alamos project, again a not uncommon situation for a Jew in his time. Does it matter that Heshie is Jewish,
even though he gives no specific thought to his religion? Of course
it does: his father became the man he was—a scientist who finally
abandoned his work on the atomic bomb for reasons of conscience—within a moral and historical context in which his background played a decisive part. He was a Jew in American history;
he was not anonymous.)

Of course I wish American Jews knew more about their religion—what I would call their Judaism, as opposed to their Jewishness, which is cultural; studied their history, knew Hebrew and
Yiddish. But I wish those for a lot of reasons; I am not really sure
how much knowing these things would change our fiction today.
One's writing comes out of the whole of oneself, and the more one
concentrates on some things the less one concentrates on others.
But our lives as Jews and Americans, as men and women, are very
complex, and we are pulled at one moment in one direction and at
another in a different one. The fact that I keep a kosher kitchen
does not always or even often affect my choice of subject matter,
let alone my technical choices.

Nor, frankly, do I want it to. Just as, a woman writer, I feel
blessedly free these days to write about any subject, any character
I can imagine, so, a Jewish writer, I do not want to issue myself a
kind of edict that will make me apologetic if I find my material,
sometimes, outside my life as a Jew. I need to pray for a long
enough life in which to do both. (Hugh Nissenson's most recent
novel is the diary of the ur-goyishche character, a man named
Thomas Keene who traveled to Ohio in the year 1812. Max Apple's
is about Howard Johnson and Walt Disney. My own, predictably
or not, is this time concerned with a piece of Jewish history, the
Am Olam movement that brought men and women from Russia
near the end of the nineteenth century; they knew nothing about
farming and did very badly at it.) As I said, one has to hope to live
long enough to do some of many kinds of things. I wish we would
hear from Israeli writers about whether they sometimes choose to
write about their cats, or about sexual rapture, or the way a soccer

ball reverberates against their foot. I assume they do, even in the fraught atmosphere of their embattled situation, but I can't even guess whether it causes them anxiety to look away, for a while at least, from politics. The question is not so dissimilar from the one I am trying to raise about our obligations as Jewish writers—just how self-conscious ought we to be when we go in search of subjects? Should the word *ought* even be spoken by writers? And if we do allow it, how can our fiction best represent the unending transformations taking place in our lives as American Jews, a hyphenated existence in which we resemble, but are still not wholly interchangeable with, our neighbors?

Meanwhile, to return to *Tikkun* as it tries to define contemporary Jewish writing. If, say, Melville were out there today and chose to send a chapter of *Moby Dick* to us, would we print it? We might, no matter what Mr. Melville's provenance, on the grounds that as Jews we have a pretty well-seasoned interest in judgment, vengeance, powerful faceless forces, and passionate commitments to rid the world of evil, especially when they're couched in biblical cadences. If the good story is, as I've suggested, amphibian, then perhaps the whale comes close enough. Certainly we would urge Mr. Melville to try his work on us, stamped, self-addressed envelope included.

# Section B
## The Israeli Context

# Polemos and Polemics

## Ruth Almog

Anyone familiar with Greek philosophy will remember the pre-Socratics and their indefatigable search for the one single explanation of all things—an explanation at once ultimate, exclusive, and all-embracing. Thales of Miletus, among others, sought it in a primordial element of substance, like water. Anaximander, somewhat younger Milesian, referred to his primal substance as *apeiron* or the Infinite, while Anaximenes, the youngest of the Milesians, favored air. As time went on, it became clear that one single element would not do and elements in combination were suggested, such as Xenophanes' water and earth, or the famous foursome: water, air, earth, and fire. With the passage of time, a more abstract underlying principle was broached such as Democritus's atomism or the Pythagorians' *harmonia,* that is, the principle of numbers, or Plato's theory of ideas.

Human beings have never given up this search for the single underlying principle or cause. It is as if our minds were structured according to a universal model, fueled by one insatiable urge: to find the most elementary, concise, and irrevocable explanation for everything, like the Big Bang, for example. And so, when I was asked to speak about the imaginative fiction written by some women in Israel today, I found myself pushed into the corner where that insatiable urge prevails—where scientists, philosophers, and literary critics gather, where the frantic search goes on for that underlying principle which will explain everything—once and for all—and for which one must amass all the supporting evidence.

There does exist, however, alongside this mode of thinking, another mode. It is perhaps more a mode of behavior than of thinking. In any case, it is predicated on the need to destroy the unifying and all-inclusive principle. It chooses, rather, to stick with the facts, to insist upon them, to endow them with importance and significance. One might say that is a mode of behavior which takes its cue from the maxim that God reveals Himself in small things. It is the behavioral mode of the artist whose entire life revolves around the need to work with details: to discover them, to examine them, to illuminate them—even if they are as meager and as insignificant as the *petite madeleines*. The artist opens the door to small details, to the poor insignificant facts, inviting them in and then weaving them into as large and colorful and exciting a tapestry as possible.

Thus, details, which serve the scientist only as means to enable him or her to construct his underlying principle—are for the artist an end in themselves: the artist conceives of the world as a mass of details. It is not the unifying principle he or she seeks in them but the world that they convey.

Since my work attaches me to this latter mode, to dealing in details, my presentation here has forced me—so to speak—to graze in foreign pastures. I must abandon the particular for the general. I must, in fact, betray myself and everything I stand for. But I will make the effort and if I fail, I, at least, can blame it on my infidelity.

In order to arrive at some underlying theory or common denominator about Hebrew prose written by women in Israel today, I would like to return to the pre-Socratic philosophers.

The Greek philosopher from Ephesus, Heraclitus "the obscure," held the view that war was "the father of all and the king of all, polemos panton men pater esti." He used the word *war* as a metaphor for opposites since he considered the universe to be composed of a great variety of opposites: sleep-wakefulness, night-day, dry-wet, etc. One wonders why he metaphorized this idea as *war*.

It is interesting to note that the Greek word *polemos*—war— appeared in Hebrew with certain changes in pronunciation and denotation. *Polemos* became *pulmus*—controversy or polemic, that is, verbal warfare. Just as one might be sorely tempted to attribute Heraclitus's metaphorical use of the word *war* (for the touchstone of existence) to his own experience of unending war, or Thales's choice of water to the fact that during his visit to Egypt, he became aware of that country's overwhelming dependence on the waters of the Nile, one is tempted to attribute the change wrought in the meaning of the word *pulmus* when it entered the Hebrew language to the prevailing reality of Jewish life at the time. But one is even more tempted to speculate on another possibility, that if words were still transferred today from the Greek to the Hebrew, the meaning of the word *polemos* would not have changed: it would have become a synonym for the word *milhama*—war—among modern Hebrew speakers. The reason is self-evident: the central experience in the life of the Israelis during the past forty years has been—war.

I mentioned before that it goes against my natural grain to seek a common denominator among women writers in Israel today. Nonetheless, I can't help realizing that there is a common denominator—if not in their prose at least in their fate. In addition to the fact that like women writers everywhere, their private experience is different from that of men, there is a central and significant aspect of life in Israel from which women are barred. I as a woman do not go to war. I as a woman have no direct experience of war. But even more, I as a woman have no way of knowing anything real or firsthand about war. I have no details—and it is in details that God reveals Himself. No woman in Israel has a martial *petite madeleine*. My experience of war comes from the newspapers, from television, not from my senses, not from touch or sound or sight—which are the real tools of the writer.

Interestingly enough, a woman writer can imagine what it's like to work in intelligence. Shulamit Hareven wrote a credible and rather successful spy story under an assumed name. But war, the battlefield? That's an entirely different matter and an entirely male experience. I don't even understand the *name* of Yehoshua Kenez's book—*Hitganvut Yehidim,* in which this experience is described. For me war is a no-man's land, excuse me, a no-woman's land.

When I was a small child, my father used to take me to the synagogue with him every Friday night. I sat next to him in the men's section and we prayed from the same *siddur*. I was aware, however, and from a very early age, that this delightful arrangement could not last forever, that it would end as soon as I reached the age of twelve. At that time I would have to leave my father's side and—if I wanted to continue to pray in the synagogue—move into the women's section. In other words, at age twelve I would be forced to leave the wonderful world of my father or, if you like, the world of men. Amalia Kahane Carmon has used this situation metaphorically to describe the situation of women writers in Israel: holy worship is performed by men in the men's section. The women are in a special enclosure, separated by a wall or a curtain, and their voices are not heard. Great things are beyond their province. Kahane Carmon further pointed out that this situation spills over into criticism and research. The woman writer is located beyond the pale, and subsequently can deal only with marginal issues.

There is an element of truth in this. Because of the limitations of her experience in one of the country's major areas of involvement, the woman writer is unable to embrace the entirety of national life. She is pushed into those areas considered less significant. The scope of her writing is confined to family life, fe-

male experience, relations between the sexes, and so forth. Thus
she affirms what Rachel the poet wrote: "Only about myself can I
speak / Narrow is my world as that of the ant." Her writing does
not deal with political questions or with great social issues. She
will never write the Israeli version of *War and Peace.* Thus, that
turning point in the history of Israel, the Six-Day War does not
reflect itself in women's writing. And typically, when I wanted to
deal with it in my book *Death in the Rain,* I chose to describe the
impact of that war on our lives from a domestic point of view. I
tried to describe what was so painful to me—the change of values
in the Israeli society after the war, by describing the change that
took place in architecture—the new kitsch villas that were being
built all over the country in the bad taste of Hollywood films, show-
ing of pink toilets and Italian marble floors; or the change in eating
habits—quite a feminine way of looking at things I would say. It is
worth remarking that the woman writer is retreating into the short
story. There she can deal with the everyday, the quotidian life.
Yehudith Handel wrote two novels when she was younger, and no
more. Amalia Kahane Carmon wrote one. Shulamit Hareven wrote
one. I am talking about women writers who have already passed
the age of fifty. Their main output is the short story. I can think of
only four notable outstanding novels produced by women writers
in recent years. Two were written by Shulamith Lapid, who re-
treated into history, and though she dealt with the national question, dealt with it only through the prism of history. I have written
the other two. In one I also tried to deal with the great questions
but again through the use of history and not through the reality of
the present. In the same way, Shulamit Hareven, in a novella, tried
to touch upon questions of national importance, stepping way back
to the most remote of times in the life of the nation.

So there they are, Israeli women writers, enclosed in the
women's section of the Temple, barricading themselves within the
confines of the short story and turning their guns on human nature.
They are writing about people, not about society. They are writing
about the individual, either because that is what interests them or
because that is what they have been left with. And their individual
is usually a woman.

But there is another side to this so-called confinement. With their
wings ostensibly clipped vis-à-vis subject matter, they have taken
wing in another direction: they have proved to be daring in literary
innovativeness. The outstanding example of this is Amalia Kahane
Carmon in her latest volume of stories. If women can't achieve
quantity, they can aim at achieving quality. One can see this not

only in their readiness to experiment but also in the daring they employ in describing the pain and suffering of everyday life. Their pencil point is sharper and they have penetrated more deeply into the human experience—illness, death, madness, servitude, the stuff of their prose.

Permit me now a more personal note. Kahane Carmon entitled one of her many lectures on women writers, "She's a Pretty Good Writer—but Marginal." She was of course referring to the way she herself had been classified, and I would like to say, parenthetically, that she is not a "pretty good" writer but a great writer. In any case, I myself have always been conscious of the stigma of female marginality. I knew that no matter how well I wrote, the stigma would remain. I would never be able to gatecrash the world of men writers. On the other hand, as I matured as a writer, I realized with growing intensity that if my artistic efforts were not also an act of subversion—in the broadest sense of the word—I would not be satisfied. This realization dawned on me as I wrote, when I began to understand the forces compelling me to write. So the stigma of marginality, on the one hand, and the idea of subversion on the other, motivated me to produce my last novel, *Shorshei Avir*. Whatever one can say about it, it does not deal with marginal issues. True, it is historical in a certain sense but even so it attempts to deal with the larger issues. And despite the fact that the protagonist is a woman, living in a decidedly woman's world, it aspires fundamentally—and openly—to be a male novel, a political one.

In conclusion, I would like to point out that the number of women writers in Israel has been growing in the last few years by leaps and bounds. The old ratio of two to one no longer holds. And if it is true that they are—for the most part—writing short stories, they are still an encouraging source of promise.

# Six Forgotten Pioneers of Hebrew Literature

## Hillel Halkin

As a Hebrew-English translator, it is natural for me to do now what I have been doing much of my life; that is, to seek to speak in English for others who are unable to do so for themselves. I would like, then, to say a few words about a group of late nineteenth- and early twentieth-century Eastern European Hebrew authors I feel especially close to and that is, for all practical purposes, unknown to English readers. There are, I believe, several reasons why this is so, one being that while it is not particularly difficult to find publishers in English for the work of living Hebrew writers—sometimes, I am inclined to think, not quite difficult enough—it is all but impossible to find them for the dead, who are not perceived as being a marketable asset. However, I hope that in some small measure this situation will be remedied by an English anthology I am currently working on—with the kind assistance of the National Endowment for the Humanities—that will include six long works of fiction by the six authors I am thinking of.

These six men (Mendele, Feierberg, Berdichevsky, Bialik, Brenner, and Gnessin—the last of whom, Bialik, died in 1934) are, as I say, unknown names in America; but the fact of the matter is that in Israel too, outside of departments of Hebrew literature, they are little more than known names, part of a consignment of cultural baggage that is rarely opened for use. Bialik, of course, as befits a "national poet," is heavily taught in the schools, where he is as effectively deadened for young readers as are the Bible, the Midrash, and other components of the Jewish literary heritage by a devastatingly textbookological approach; Brenner has undergone a minor revival, perhaps because the sole member of this group to live in Palestine and write about life there, he is the only one whose attitudes seem recognizably proto-Israeli to an audience that has difficulty relating to the world of East-European Jewish culture; all the others are little more than subjects for matriculation exams. In this sense, some of the remarks that follow about what I believe to be the contemporary Jewish relevance of these figures—a relevance related, but by no means restricted, to their strictly literary achievements—might be addressed to an Israeli audience too.

But how, you ask, can one generalize so sweepingly, either here or in Israel, about a group of writers who (for they could hardly be serious authors if they were not) are highly individuated in their work? The answer to this reasonable question, I think tells us something significant about East-European Hebrew literature as a whole. For if it would be absurd to try drawing a "typical" bio-graphical or literary profile of the late nineteenth- or early twen-tieth-century French or English author—what really, after all, does Huysmans have to do with Zola, or Conrad with Joyce?—this is not at all the case with Hebrew. On the contrary: one of the unique characteristics of East-European Hebrew writing is that it was done by writers who came from highly similar backgrounds and shared so much common experience that their more autobiographi-cal work sometimes reads as if it were written about a single life. Essentially, this is so because writing secular Hebrew literature in a society where the Hebrew language was not spoken and was for the most part used only in a sacral context was an anomalous act to begin with, one that presupposed several things. First, it meant being subjected as a child and adolescent to the extreme rigors of a traditional Jewish Orthodox education, which alone could pro-vide a young man (women, of course, were automatically excluded from the process) with the facility in Hebrew that might enable him to put the language to literary use. (Although the claim is some-times made that an extensive schooling was near universal among male Jews in Eastern Europe, this was hardly the case; most boys were given only the bare rudiments of a religious education, while serious Talmudic and rabbinic studies, which means spending the equivalent of today's high-school and college years at a yeshiva, an institute of rabbinical learning, were reserved for a small elite.) Second, it then meant breaking with this background intellectually and emotionally, since the rabbinical student who remained in the Orthodox fold would never think of literature as a career. Third, however, it meant not breaking so radically that one left the Jewish community altogether, in which case there would be no point in writing in Hebrew at all. And last, it meant choosing Hebrew, a language that most East-European Jews could not read on a literary level, over its far more accessible Jewish alternative of Yiddish—a choice that commonly went together with an anti-Diaspora Zionism

and an elitist approach to Jewish culture in general, just as opting
for Yiddish most often implied a non- or even anti-Zionist cultural populism.

Thus, all of the six authors I have mentioned passed through
many of the same way-stations in life. All except Mendele, who
belongs to an earlier generation, were born in the last quarter of
the nineteenth century into a pious, lower-middle-class family in a
heavily Jewish shtetl in Czarist Russia. (It was such families that
most often turned to a rabbinic education as a means of advancing
their children, since the well-off had less arduous options and the
very poor had to put their sons to work.) All attended the local
heder or schoolroom for long hours and years, and then left home
as adolescents to continue their studies at a yeshiva. All broke
with religion in late adolescence or early adulthood after a period
of inner turmoil that culminated in a rupture, or the threat of one,
with their families and social environment. All continued even after
this to maintain their intense Jewish loyalties. All began writing
fiction (or, in the case of Bialik, poetry) in Hebrew because, despite
their loss of faith, years of religious training had made it the language they felt culturally and personally most at home in. And all
either became committed Zionists or struggled with the reasons
they felt they couldn't be. Indeed, to be a Hebrew author without
a belief in Zionism was to live a conscious contradiction in terms
(although one that writers like Mendele or Gnessin proved quite
capable of living), since only the success of Zionism, with its call
for the revival of Hebrew as a national language, could guarantee
a future audience for one's own work. In effect, the very act of
writing in Hebrew was, for such men, simultaneously a repudiation
of, and an act of faith in, the Jewish world that they had grown
up in.

Moreover, in addition to this congruence in their private lives,
the writers I am speaking of shared a public agenda. Indeed, private and public concerns were hardly distinguishable for them,
since the same crisis of religious faith and social tradition that each
had experienced individually was also—less articulately—affecting
the entire Jewish world around them. And because they were not
only at the forefront of this process in a personal sense, but the
one force capable of giving it public expression, since apart from
its increasingly out-of-touch rabbinical leadership, East-European
Jewry had no intelligentsia or recognized spokesmen apart from
its literary figures, writing in Hebrew during this period meant
shouldering a collective burden that one was not at liberty to put
down. Willy-nilly, early modern Hebrew literature is ridden, even

when chafing angrily against it, with an almost overwhelming sense of social responsibility; and inasmuch as its authors were all confronting the same issues, they were not only all reading each other, but all addressing each other as well. This is especially so because, for all its sense of public mission, the world of Hebrew culture was a tiny one. We are talking, all in all, about an embattled literary vanguard, a handful of serious authors, most of them personally acquainted, and a small number of dedicated readers; so that the whole enterprise, with its smattering of Hebrew journals and publishers, had about it an almost intimate family air. It is this sense of being cloistered *en famille* that helps give the Hebrew writing of this period its peculiar ingrown passion, its intense love-hate relationship with the society it springs from and describes. In a state of radical tension between negation and affirmation, writers like Mendele, Berdichevsky, Bialik, Feierberg, Gnessin, and Brenner are all, each in his own manner, split souls for whom Hebrew, ambiguously pointing backward to a world of faith outgrown and forward to a Jewish life transvalued, and literature, with its ability to accommodate otherwise irreconcilable opposites, are ways, if not of becoming whole again, at least of preventing themselves from being torn even more tragically apart.

Rebellion—exile—the exorbitant price of lost innocence—the radical loneliness of the human condition: these are the themes that occur again and again in these men's work. At first glance it may seem paradoxical that a body of writing so closely linked with a movement of national renaissance should be at the same time so ridden with private despair; yet the paradox is explained by the social origins of the writers involved. Both heirs of, and arch-rebels against, the rabbinical tradition that produced them, they have about them a Luciferian pride, defiance, and guilt that sets them apart not only from that tradition, but from the rank-and-file of their own people whose revolutionary leaders they purport to be. Often, indeed—in their literary crudition, in the elitism of their concern with issues of cultural identity and cultural authority, in the fierce religious longing of their godlessness—they seem to internalize permutations of rabbinic attitudes that they themselves are unaware of harboring. An isolated hieratic class in a world that they themselves helped desacralize, they are the most tragically lonely of men; little wonder, then, that human loneliness figures so prominently in their work. It is a loneliness both social and existential, social because existential, as Hofni, the young protagonist of Feierberg's novella *Whither?* realizes. Standing together with his father in the synagogue on the fast day of Tisha b'Av, whose mourning for the destruction of the Temple is paralleled by his own sense of devastation over the ruined temple of faith in his heart, he cries out:

> Give me back my God, the God of the Jews! The God of Aristotle can do nothing for me. Give me back the God who is near to me and I to Him! The God of Abraham, Isaac and Jacob, the God of Moses and the Prophets, the God of all this holy congregation. . . . Take what you want from me—heaven and hell, my share in the world to come—but give me back my light, my soul, my heart, my people, my God!

Hofni knows that the punishment for losing his God is the biblical *karet,* being cut off from his people, and it may be said of many of the Hebrew writers of this period, and certainly of men like Feierberg, Brenner, Berdichevsky, and Bialik, that their literary careers were partly aimed at establishing a new community of readers to replace the community of worshipers that was lost.

And indeed, establish it for a short while they did—in Warsaw, in Vilna, in Odessa, in New York, in Jerusalem, in little towns and villages throughout Eastern Europe; for the readers who read them came too from similar backgrounds and led the same generational lives. Perhaps never before or again in the history of modern literature has so strong a bond existed between writer and reader, even if the latter's numbers never exceeded a few tens of thousands, many of whom did not buy the books they read, since copies commonly passed from hand to hand. During the brief lives of the literary figures they closely followed—Feierberg was dead at twenty-five, Gnessin at thirty-four, Brenner at forty, Berdichevsky at fifty-six—they constituted as receptive and responsive an audience as any author could wish for.

This elite, international community of Hebrew letters, short-lived to begin with, is gone and unreconstitutable. Yet its disintegration, which was already complete half a century ago, is not the only barrier between us and its literature, nor the only reason that the latter's translation has yet to arouse our interest. In reading modern East-European Hebrew writing today we have to deal not only with the vast gap between its world and ours, or with its sometime serious aesthetic imperfections that did not much bother readers more immediately concerned with the interpretation of experience than with its aestheticization, but with yet another problem: namely, with this writing's relationship to its own subject matter.

In a word, the Hebrew literature of this period is a literature of intense ambivalence—and ours is not, I think, an age that values ambivalence highly, not in general, and certainly not in regard to our Jewishness. We live in prophylactic times that have taught us to think of unresolved emotional conflict as the seedbed of crippling neuroses, an immature stage of personal development that needs to be worked through, and the Catullan *odi et amo* does not strike us as a hygienic proposition, especially when what we love and hate is within us, forming part of our socially conditioned ego; while as Jews, that is, as a people that has been the object of such pathological enmity in this century, we cannot help but regard the slightest sign of self-hatred in our midst, no matter how balanced it is by its opposite, with fear and apprehension. If we choose to be Jews, we wish to be proud ones in the face of our enemies, whom we do not wish to see within our gates; and an Oedipal duality toward tradition, a deep longing for its protective warmth that rages against its restrictive limits, may seem to us a literary Trojan horse that we have every reason to suspect. At the very least, the self-lacerating quality of such writing makes it painful for us to read, for its authors are wounding themselves each time they stab at Jewry and what they write is written with their blood.

And yet in speaking as a translator in their behalf, permit me to say a few words in behalf of ambivalence, of Jewish ambivalence, too.

These men were not, in their work (their lives, of course, are something else) neurotic: if they both loved and hated the world from which they sprang, and sometimes did so with a savagery that may shock us ("the Jews," Mendele is once reported to have said, "are shit, but what can I do if that's the very substance I happen to carry around in my own guts?"), this was because there was indeed much to be loved and hated in that world itself, to which ambivalence was a fully natural reaction, perhaps the only possible integration of emotions toward a birthright so contradictory. How could one not love the Jewish world of Eastern Europe for its warmth, its faith, its intelligence, its steadfastness, its vitality? How could one not hate it for its fanaticism, its contentiousness, its narrow-mindedness, its self-deludedness, its pitiful arrogance toward everything outside it? Most Jews, of course, did one or another, either clinging to this world or abandoning it with sufficient singlemindedness to preserve their simple sense of inner unity. But singlemindedness, while sometimes useful in daily life, is not the stuff from which great literature is made. The ability to accommodate in a single soul mutually antagonistic perceptions may or may not be the beginning of wisdom; it is certainly the beginning of serious fiction.

This may be stating the obvious; in any case, it is not saying nearly enough. If we are content to historicize early modern Hebrew literature—if we say merely, "Oh, yes, it had to fight its way out of the shtetl, what a terrible emotional battle that was!"—by which we also mean, of course, "How fortunate that we are already beyond all that!"—we are missing the point. For the point is that we are not beyond it at all; a deep ambivalence toward tradition remains the contemporary condition of *every* contemporary Jewish intellectual who has not simply turned his back on the enterprise of being Jewish, and acknowledging as much is the first prerequisite for confronting tradition in good faith. This is so because, whatever our sense of Jewishness may be, it includes a uniquely modern insistence on the right to self-definition that tradition itself cannot possibly grant us; and in seeking to apply this right to tradition, to wrest from it an identity that is our own, we are of necessity rebelling against it in the very act of engaging it. This act has about it something illicit, Promethean, as is always the case when we steal divine fire to warm our human selves; and such a theft must arouse in us a complexity of emotions, among which we are likely to identify not only the satisfaction of conquest, but also the remorse of betrayal. There can be nothing singleminded about such a relationship. We may not be coming from the same place as Brenner and Berdichevsky, but we are still traveling on the same road; and though we have left the shtetl behind us, we have not left behind its passions, its divisions, or even some of its aberrancies, as the two days of this conference have shown us.* A heightened sense of ambivalence in regard to our own Jewishness might not only help us to read the writers I have spoken of with greater appreciation; it might better balance that within us which is self-righteously defensive with that which is uncharitably self-accusing; it might protect us from the tendency to think that the struggle is always with others, never with ourselves; and it might, I think, help us to cope with the enormous riches and limitations of Jewishness without losing our emotional completeness, our critical faculties, our sense of perspective, or even our sense of humor.

The body of Hebrew writing that I have been speaking of, it should

---

*At this point in the conference proceedings, which had unexpectedly turned out to be more about politics than literature, an acrimonious debate had broken out between two factions of participants. One, in the name of the struggle for Israel and Jewish survival, was attacking the "self-hate" in Jewish and Israeli literature that undermines Jewish solidarity and aids the foe; the other, in the name of the Jewish writer's moral conscience, was attacking the first group as if *it* were the foe. The pall of the intifada hung heavily over the conference hall. It would have taken a Brenner to do full justice to the absurdity of the scene.

be clear by now, is a literature of religious crisis. Today, when— or at least such is my personal impression—the question of religious faith is of equally little concern to most observant and nonobservant Jews alike (in speaking of observant Jews, of course, I am not referring to that considerable segment of Orthodoxy which is living in the twentieth century in a calendary sense only), we are likely to see early modern Hebrew literature's obsessive preoccupation with the consequences of lost faith as the dramatization of an adolescent problem that the dramatizer was unable to outgrow. If we do, however, I think we will be wrong. We may have arrived, religious and secular Jews together, at a comfortable and intellectually rationalized praxis to which the question of ultimate beliefs seems irrelevant, but this belief in the irrelevancy of belief reminds me of a remark once made by Kierkegaard. The reason, Kierkegaard writes somewhere, that in ancient times faith could move mountains while nowadays it moves nothing at all, and so appears a superfluity, is that once faith was highly difficult to attain and thus represented a genuine achievement, whereas now that Kant and Hegel have proven the existence of God, it is so easily arrived at by everyone that it is of little account. Does it really make a difference if what seems to have been proven in our century is the opposite?

If I may resort to the language of parable, the Hebrew writers I am speaking of are comparable to men who, having ridden through a deep forest, came to an endlessly wide and yawning abyss, peered astonishedly down into it, concluded that they could not cross it, dismounted from their horses, and went about for the rest of their lives on foot with an overwhelming sense of vertigo, to which they gave literary expression. Today, not a few Jews, I think, are back in the forest again, walking at a safe enough distance parallel to the abyss for it to be out of sight, yet with the comfortable illusion of having already crossed over to the other side. This illusion is possible because, never having stared into the abyss themselves, they have no idea of how wide and deep it is, or of what crossing it, were such a thing possible, might entail. "Those who are unhappy to find themselves without faith, show us that God does not enlighten them; but the others show us that there is a God who is blinding them." These words are Pascal's, although they could just as well have been the Rabbi of Kotsk's; I would merely add to them the observation that by "the others," Pascal meant to refer to two quite different categories of people. In their refusal to be blinded by God, Hebrew writers like Feierberg, Gnessin, Brenner, and Berdichevsky paradoxically belong, I think, to the Jewish religious tradition that we shall all have to continue to grapple with.

# On the Predominance of Poetry in Modern Hebrew Literature

## Meir Wieseltier

Before I go ahead, I would like to share with you a certain inescapable embarrassment I suffer at having to use English, or, for that matter, any other foreign language, when I am supposed to speak of any aspect that has to do with Hebrew poetry. This embarrassment has nothing to do with my admittedly limited mastery of English. I would be quite happy to use my awkward English on any other subject.

You may find my feelings rather peculiar in a world where English has established itself for some time as a *lingua franca,* in which all subjects may be usefully discussed, and where translation, and the transmitting of ideas through translation, has become one of the main thoroughfares of intellectual communication on a global scale. But I am stuck with the uneasy apprehension that this happy state of affairs does not really apply to Hebrew poetry. In fact, there is some obvious difficulty in discussing aspects of any poetry in a language other than the one it was written in. But this universal difficulty can be overcome, or at least mitigated, if your audience is conversant with that poetry in a variety of extant translations, and has a real measure of intimacy with the mental climate and the intellectual context it springs from. Hebrew poetry cannot profit from such mitigation for a host of reasons, the most simple as well as the most frustrating of which is the lack of a considerable body of first-rate translations of the Hebrew poets into any language, English being no exception. So Hebrew poetry remains a *terra incognita,* an almost closed book, *k'sefer ha'chatum,* to those who don't read the language. And as I happen to believe that poetry should be talked about from within, the very fact that I'm talking of Hebrew poetry in English makes me feel a bit funny. But let's leave it at that.

Anyone who is at all familiar with modern Hebrew literature will notice the special standing enjoyed by poetry in that literature all along. This special standing, or predominance, has many aspects, both quantitative and qualitative. The quantitative ones are the easiest to single out. The sheer number of poetry books, and their percentage in the overall literary production in Hebrew, is, or used to be, until quite recently, wildly abnormal, if compared with what we know from other literatures. So are the sales numbers. A new novel by an established writer may sell only twice as many copies as a new volume by a well-known poet. When it comes to best sellers, prose does of course have larger reserves of random readers, so a poetry best seller will sell only about a quarter of its prose counterpart, which is still very striking if compared with proportions on other book markets. So is the sheer number of poets in the literary community. They probably outnumber prose writers, and I am talking of published poets. It is true no Hebrew poet can make a living, even a meager one, from his poetry, but then only a tiny number of novelists can. In Israel poets feature on radio and television, and in the written press, on a scale undreamt of in other countries. This stems from the fact that poetry and poets have some kind of celebrity status in the community at large. Even journalists read poetry, and in the Israeli press you will sometimes find headlines that are shaped after lines from contemporary poems. The man on the street, even if he is no great reader of books, is quite familiar with the best-known Hebrew poets of the day, at least by name.

Another aspect of this abnormality is the special function of poetry and poets in the development and growth of modern Hebrew literature throughout this century. In the second half of the nineteenth century, modern Hebrew literature evolved mainly in the Czar's empire, side by side with Yiddish literature, and in the proximity of Russian literature. In both of them, at the time, prose was the unquestioned queen of literature. But in modern Hebrew literature, from Yalag and certainly from Bialik onward, the hierarchy was reversed. Poetry won the day and became the vanguard, the trend setter, and the pride of modern Hebrew literature. Succeeding literary generations were named, both by literary critics and by the public at large, after their eminent poets rather than after their prose counterparts. This trend became even more pronounced as the literary center gradually shifted from Russia to Palestine. The literary generation of Bialik and Tschernichovsky was eventually succeeded by that of Shlonsky and Alterman as the high priests of literature, while the literary opposition to those trend setters was also headed by poets, Grinberg and Ratosh. The

greatest prose writers of the first half of the twentieth century—
Gnesin, Brenner, and then Agnon—had no generations named after
them, and headed no schools. Shlonsky and Alterman ruled su-
preme for decades, and the writers of the 1940s, both poets *and
novelists,* commonly known as *dor ha'polemikh,* saw themselves
as their disciples. When they finally gave way, it was again to a
group of poets that appeared on the scene in the 1950s—Amichai,
Zach, and Avidan, later joined by Dahlia Ravikovitch. And the next
literary opening was once again the work of poets, the so-called
poets of the 1960s—Hurwitz, Wollach, and myself. It is important
to stress that this unusual state of affairs was not caused by sheer
literary power-politics or the formation of literary power-politics
or the formation of literary cliques. The main *raison d'être* of this
state of affairs was that poets were indeed the main innovators and
builders of modern Hebrew literature. They were its legislators.
They were the first to introduce new subject matter, new spiritual
or intellectual standpoints and new affiliations with influences from
foreign literatures. And, besides, most of the time we simply had
a far greater number of first-rate poets than of first-rate novelists.
So you had a phenomenon of poetic hegemony that no longer existed in other literatures. So when A. B. Yehoshua was asked in
an interview about the formative influences on his early work, he
named poets of the 1950s and 1960s rather than novelists, and he
was quite right in doing so.

When, as a young man, I first went abroad, I arrived in London,
where I was introduced to some well-educated people. Some of
them were journalists, some architects, some students of Slavonic
literatures. I was amazed to find out that none of them had a ready
answer to my simple question: Who are your favorite contemporary English poets? My new friends simply read no contemporary
poetry. Indeed, since they have left school, they weren't in the habit
of reading poetry at all. But they were all avid readers of prose
and knew all about the latest novels. That is how I first discovered
how unusual was the state of affairs in my own native literature.

Later, I found out that many people had noticed it, but I never
came across a serious attempt to explain it. My own explanations
at the time were based on three main points. They had to do with
the old Hebrew literary heritage, with the birth pangs of the revival
of Hebrew as a modern language, and with the formative phase of
modern Hebrew literature in its Russian literary environment.

First, I argued, in the pioneering generations of modern Hebrew
literature, the Hebrew poets stood on much firmer ground than the
Hebrew prose writers. They had behind them a much more solid,

or at least richer tradition to refer to. They were backed by an age-old, though fragmented heritage of poetry in Hebrew. Besides the Bible, which has a treasure of poetry and of poetic ideas, as well as a richness of myth and allusion, they had the later *pitanim,* the *siddur,* or Hebrew prayerbook, and the whole body of Hebrew poetry written in Spain in the early centuries of this millennium. In short, they had a great complex of extant traditions to refer to and to work from, and did so, crossing it with various modern European influences. The Hebrew prose writer had very little in comparison.

Second, the revival of Hebrew, the initial effort to forge it into a modern vehicle for secular literature, provided the poet with a much better tool than it did the storyteller. Modern Hebrew emerged, especially at its early stages, as an idiom much better suited for poetry. It lacked too many things that are essential to a fully developed prose, both in its vocabulary and in its modes of expression. It is also terribly difficult, I think, to the point of bordering with the absurd, to write a narrative in a language not used by its readership in daily life, in their bedrooms, and in the marketplace. Hebrew writers in Odessa and Warsaw, as well as Berlin, did it nevertheless; they wrote Hebrew prose, and translated into Hebrew masterpieces of world literature and from Yiddish. But they had to surmount enormous difficulties, and they could hardly keep up with the quality and depth of the new poetic idiom, which developed faster.

Third, though the peaks of Russian literature in the late nineteenth century were novels, novellas, and short stories, rather than poetry, Russians were still great readers of poetry, both native and translated. Then, on the brink of the twentieth century and in its first decades, there was a great breakthrough in Russian poetry, with the symbolists, the acemists and the futurists. Poetry reasserted itself once again, and young Hebrew writers such as Shlonsky, Rachel, or Lea Goldberg, as well as their potential readers, grew up in the midst of this poetic revolution, and later on carried its spirit and its reading habits to the new settlements in Palestine.

To this a fourth factor must be added. The development of modern Hebrew literature is practically inseparable from the Jewish national revival in Eastern Europe, from the *chevet tzion* movement, and later on from Zionism and from the succeeding waves of *aliyah.* This kind of national revival and upheaval probably makes more room for poetry and polemics than it does for a narrative prose.

In light of all this, one could expect to see a constant strengthening of prose as the Hebrew literary scene gradually shifted to Palestine. The *yishuv* in Eretz Israel and the immigrants who later became the Israelis, at last gave modern Hebrew literature those long-hoped-for native readers, readers whose main or even only spoken language was modern Hebrew. Spoken Hebrew developed at a pace unparalleled by any other attempted renewal of a dormant languge. Indeed, at an amazing pace. And Jewish history in the twentieth century could provide the novelist and the storyteller with a terrible treasure of unprecedented situations, plots, and characters. Moreover, most Hebrew speakers in the first half of this century were quite new at it, and their mastery of it was far from complete. So the easier idiom of prose could suit them much better than the denser and more elliptical idiom of poetry. It was reasonable to expect a gradual ascendence of prose over poetry in the new Hebrew literature written in Eretz Israel, and later in Israel.

But in reality, the very opposite happened. For some mysterious reason, Eretz Israel seemed to prove an arid soil for prose. Not so much in quantity—for we had many novelists and short-story writers in the first half of this century—but certainly in literary value and complexity. There was something rather stilted in most of the Hebrew prose written during the thirties, the forties, and the fifties. In fact, decade after decade, poetry became even more central than in the former, European centers of modern Hebrew literature. Our best texts of Hebrew prose came from writers who lived the first half of their lives, or at least its formative phases, in their countries of origin, rather than in Eretz Israel. The old-new native soil produced no prose to match their achievements. Hebrew prose seemed to have very little to offer after Brenner, Shoffman, Reuveni, Agnon, or even Yaakov Steinberg and Berkovitz. Moreover, while poetry managed to innovate without losing its depth, and to keep in touch with new trends in world poetry, the new Hebrew prose writers, from the thirties onward, seemed unable to absorb even the achievements of their predecessors. Instead they got stuck with the life-killing models-the Russian social-realist novel or the old type of historical novel—and with an awkward idiom that was monstrously ill-suited to the reality they were trying to depict. There was no spirit of experiment and no spiritual depth to be found in that prose.

So now we have to pose the question a little differently: why did the development of Hebrew prose in those decades differ so much from the development of Hebrew poetry? Why did the prose writer succumb to so many pitfalls that the poet managed to avoid? My main answer to this is that poetry flourished because the loyalty of the Hebrew poet was given first and foremost to his art, to the language, and to his inner truth, while the new Hebrew prose writer was, for decades, too much of a loyal servant to the provisional ideas and ideals provided by the various spokesmen of Zionism. The Hebrew prose writer of the first generations that grew up in Eretz Israel, was never really a free and independent spirit. And many readers were quick to sense it, and it is to the poets that they looked in their search for an independent assessment of their existential fulfillment.

Of course, the story is not that simple. It is not that most prose writers happened to be spiritual cowards, while the poets were brave men and women. In the given historical situation, the difficult feat to be performed for Hebrew literature was easier for poetry. In a prose text one always depends on the time-and-locale backbone to be found in the opening sentence of Don Quixote—"At a certain village in La Mancha . . . there lived not long ago." Prose can never really dodge them. It depends on them. And it is not just a *sense* of time and place, as is sometimes found in poetry. Prose, even modernistic prose, is always some kind of history, and sometimes, the acutal history of a people is so harsh and cruel that neither prose writer nor his public has the nerve to cast a cold eye on it. History becomes a Medusa that cannot be faced. Or is faced with a lying smile. Poetry, on the other hand, can evade any historical time and meld down any locale by the means of music and by its patters of lacunae, its privileged gaps. Even a narrative poem, if it is not prose in verse, turns time into music. That is not to say that poetry lacks concreteness; it has its own brand of concreteness. But all prose is essentially stopping and looking back, an effort to relive a past or to invent one, or to try and understand something about things past. Poetry, like music, is essentially movement—it is futuristic. And by being essentially futuristic it can hover over the fire and the ashes where prose is too timid to walk. Poetry can play the burning bush.

Zionist resettlement of Palestine, and later Israel, was accompanied by a cracking break with many pasts and by the cleavage of millions of individual lives. To a large degree it had to close its eyes and turn its back on millions of individual tragedies. It is little wonder novelists did not muster the courage to stand and look back or just around them with a straight eye or to really try to understand the recent past, rather than extenuate it. It was an awful task, one for which poetry was perhaps better suited.

# Response to Wieseltier

## Amos Oz

Every literature worthy of its name is subversive in the deepest sense of the word. The prophets were subversive politically, but not only politically. It is subversive in the way of removing the truths of yesterday or the myths and stereotypes of yesterday, generating new myths and stereotypes to be, in turn perhaps, removed by another generation of writers and poets. It is an old game, and subversiveness to me is not a dirty word. Yes, Hebrew literature is subversive and I am glad it is.

Hillel Halkin was profoundly right when he stressed the element of ambivalence in what I would call the great untranslated generation of Hebrew letters: Bialik and Brenner, Berdichevsky, Gnessin and Feierberg. Agnon is a partial exception; he has been translated. Ambivalence is the key to understanding their literature, but it is also the key to understanding the later Hebrew literature—which is not to be read on the same scale and not to be treated with the same magnitude that I, personally, ascribe to that great generation of Hebrew writers. A certain theological quest has been at work everywhere in Hebrew literature, sometimes in a very overwhelming, and resounding way. Theology, not religion, is another way of looking at the broad scene of Hebrew literature.

Meir Wieseltier was also right when he said that there is an overwhelming priority, a presence, a perseverance of poetry over prose in modern Hebrew literature—at least up until recently. I am not in the business of rating the last twenty years; it is boring, and we do not have the equipment anyway. I would not mind if, in the end, it transpires that even in the last twenty years poetry is still the leading art of Hebrew letters. Yes, poetry has been prominent, but perhaps not for the reasons that Meir Wieseltier pointed out. I would say that the entire Zionist enterprise has been a poetic undertaking. The revival of the language has been a poetic undertaking. Harvey Shapiro told me that in fact it is fairly typical of any new nation or a nation at a revolutionary phase in its history for poetry to become very prominent. It is true now in many third-world nations, and it is true in all nations undergoing revolutionary changes in various times. It might have been true at some points in time in America.

In Hebrew it is not just the revolutionary national situation of the last two hunded years or so, or just the establishment of a new nation that brought poetry to prominence, but the undertaking of reviving a virtually dead language and bringing it back to life. It is difficult to use prose in a mimetic way when the language itself changes at an almost comical pace. The colloquial of today is the anachronism of tomorrow, and I mean literally tomorrow.

A few decades ago we had no colloquial at all. The mimetic Hebrew prose, to the extent that had it been written in Palestine, still related to the shtetl or to other Jewish centers. The mimetic Hebrew prose that was created in Palestine and was related to Palestine began, significantly, with Brenner; that is the only name which comes to mind which is prominent. A man who was mad enough, and raving enough, and courageous enough to use virtually a broken, shattered language in order to try to reflect or to capture a transitive reality.

An earthquake is no time for a novel. An erupting volcano is not the right scene for an epic—certainly not a mimetic epic. And these have been the living conditions of the Zionist enterprise for ten decades now.

If I had to describe in a picturesque way where the novel can thrive, I would say either in lakes or in very slow rivers, and not in waterfalls, or gushing rivers.

That we recently have a certain revival of the mimetic novel, is perhaps a syndrome of a certain consolidation that I view with mixed feelings. But my mixed feelings are not the point here. Poetry, as Meir Wieseltier suggested, doesn't have more courage or take more liberties than prose. Our prose, has not been more "committed," or "conventional." The most important Israeli born writer to this day is S. Yizhar, alias Yizhar Smilansky, who has been silent for the last twenty-nine years. Although silent on the literary scene, he is very active politically. He wrote various novellas and short stories and one major, not novel, story. One thousand, one hundred and forty-three pages, but it is still called a story, not a novel, on the title page. It takes place within five days, and it is the single most formative work of prose of modern Hebrew written by an Israeli-born writer. No other single work of literature has changed or revolutionized the Israel psyche, even vis-à-vis Zionism and Zionist conventions, more than *The Days of Ziklag* by Yizhar, and two of his relatively more familiar, and more familiar to Israelis, short stories: *Khirbet Khiza'h* and *The Prisoner.*

Now to assume that this member of the Palmach generation was, by virtue of being a prose writer, "more bound to Zionist truths," or "less courageous," is to misunderstand what happened on the scene. It is true, he was an establishment man. He was even a member of the Knesset for too many years. Each moment of his time in the Knesset was a tremendous waste of time, for him and for Hebrew literature.

Nevertheless, Yizhar is the one who opened the road to all the subversive literature that followed.

Subversive, not by being pro-Palestinian and anti-Zionist, or soft on Zionist truths; but subversive in the sense of realizing that in the Israeli-Palestinian conflict we are dealing with a tragedy and not with a Wild West film. The fulfillment of Zionism involves not just one, but a series of Greek tragedies, with clashes between right and right. I am not only referring to Jews and Palestinians; I am referring to Jews and Jews, Oriental and Ashkenazi. I am referring to Hebrew and Yiddish. I was recently reminded of that tragic confrontation, much forgotten now, in the twenties and thirties, when the Zionist leadership in Palestine was officially attempting to suppress Yiddish in order to make Hebrew prevail. Who would ever have known that this argument between Hebrew and Yiddish was to be decided by Hitler? Who wanted Hebrew to win through Hitler?

There were many such tragic confrontations and clashes between right and right, which is basically the ambivalent context of our literature all the way from the haskalah, from the very first early poets to the latest novel to appear in Tel Aviv this year.

Now if we do understand those truths, the subversiveness, the tragic realization that the reality is tragic, this does not make me personally less of a Zionist. I have realized that Zionism entails many tragedies, and I still remain a Zionist because I think non-Zionism entails even worse tragedies. And finally, yes, the predominant role of poetry manifested itself in the fact that some of us prose writers have been humbly trying to write poetic prose, not so much because we preferred poetic prose to prosaic prose, but simply because prosaic prose was immensely difficult to achieve in a new culture, in a new language, in a new reality, in a changing reality. In a language in which you use the word *peasant* and you do not even know what you are talking about.

I do not know a word of Russian, but I am sure if you uttered the word *peasant* in Russian, *muzkin,* or whatever it is, the person would appear on stage wearing his boots or leggings or whatever; you can see him, you just utter the word and there he is.

You say the Hebrew word *ikar,* and what do you see? A German Jewish intellectual kibbutznik, in whose library is a volume of the latest issue on growing cotton leaning on the latest edition of interpretations of Kafka? Is he our peasant? Or is he a Yemenite settler? Or both?

This is just one of a million examples to explain why the language is still, perhaps, in an Elizabethan era. In some ways, this is a wonderful thing to have a wonderful musical instrument to play; and in other ways, it is unruly, difficult to tackle, and, indeed, very tempting to lean toward poetry.

I have been personally struggling for many years as a prose writer to get prosaic. The moment I can look at my own pages and say, "All right, you have gotten prosaic, you have written a piece of prose, prosaic prose and not poetic prose," both I and my various translators into various languages would heave a deep sigh of relief.

# Part III
## Breaking the Language Barrier: Literary Dialogues between Israel and the Diaspora

# Introduction

## Arnold Eisen

Most of us spend a great deal of our time constructing images of others—it's how we make our way in the world. From fragments of word and gesture we infer motive and intent; from parts, we picture wholes and then go on to relate to those imagined wholes hoping thereby to authenticate what we have imagined and render it more complete.

What all of us do every day, writers do more expertly. It is their craft. They are experts in the imagination of others, and Jewish writers—writers not only Jewish by birth, but possessed of deep Jewish knowledge—emerge from a tradition in which the imagination of human others and the divine Other has been a central and sacred task.

That wider context is immediately relevant because the very words Jewish writers use, the connotations of those words, the power of words such as *exile, land, Israel* to move us, derive from the history and tradition that continue to shape us. As long as there have been Jews, we have known both home and exile.

Consider the parsha, Lech Lecha, where after a long series of generations and degenerations, we finally come to the climactic appearance of Abraham on the stage. Abraham is promised the Land of Israel. He is permitted by the narrator to remain in the land for precisely five verses before being thrust once more into exile in Egypt. He and his descendants will return to the land and leave the land again and again.

Consider more importantly that we Jews have always, from that text onward, imagined home in terms of exile and imagined exile in terms of home. When Moses, in the Book of Deuteronomy, tries to get Israelites revved up for the task of homecoming, he pictures the land of Israel as the reverse of the exile they have known in Egypt. When the rabbis, resigned to exile, sought to make sense of it, they did so by describing it as the reverse of the home they deeply longed for.

113

A hundred years ago Zionists stood in a long tradition when they pictured the state they hoped to build in Israel as the reverse of all the Jews had known and hated in the shtetl. Forty years ago David Ben Gurion, with good reason, summoned energy for the task of nation building by contrasting what would be built in Israel with the fateful drama of exile just enacted in Europe.

And today, I think, American Jews imagine their own community in terms shaped if not dictated by Israelis, while Israelis understand what it means to come home in large part by contrast with the most relevant and challenging Diaspora in the world today: that of America. Not the least of the ways in which Israelis and Diaspora Jews need each other is that we need each other for our own self-definition. We need each other to be the other for ourselves, with all the guilt and anger and depth of relation that this inevitably involves.

The following writers are steeped in this tradition, and they are well aware of it. They will, we hope, carry the discussion forward, perhaps by drastically transforming the meanings of the key terms—*home* and *exile*—in which, now as ever, it is couched.

# Imagining the Other: 1

## Amos Oz

When I was a kid in Jerusalem in the forties, I knew about only two kinds of Jews: the old kind of Jews and the new kind of Jews.

The old kind were Diaspora Jews. They had intellect but flabby muscle. They were terribly wise, but always terribly frightened. They could not and would not harm a fly because they were extremely kind people, but everyone could harm them and indeed, everyone would harm them for some reason that I did not quite understand when I was a kid, and that I understand even less, now that I have grown up.

In between one pogrom and the next, the old Jews were fiddlers, peddlers, a rag-tag lot; nonetheless, they had a way with money. They could write books, play the violin, argue on anything at all, and always win the argument. Yet they were forever terrified and uneasy, and always sad—except when they decided to be funny, which they could do frightfully well by mocking themselves. But even when they were very, very funny they were sad nonetheless.

And when they arrived in Jerusalem, these old kind of Jews, it was our duty, so I was taught, to teach them Hebrew and to help them step right out of their own skins. To be born anew, almost—the sooner the better. They had to get sun-tanned to begin with. They were, of course, highly educated, but we were to reeducate them nonetheless. They could cure cancer, create an artificial planet, or play the piano well enough to bring forbidden tears to our eyes, and yet, we were supposed to reeducate them because they could not even tie their own shoe laces—at least not without uttering some sort of lamentation.

That much for what I knew of the old kind of Jews. The new Jews were no more familiar to me, perhaps less. They were just the opposite, but I never saw them; they were not to be seen in Jerusalem. They were far away. They breed in kibbutzim, in the Palmach, in the Negev and Galilee. Always elsewhere. They were tough and blond and tender and powerful and uncomplicated. They toiled over the land all day and in the evening, made wild love to the kibbutz girls, and then later at night picked up their submachine guns, and dashed out to smash the hostile red Indians or Arabs, before calling it a day.

Now, of course, I've grown up to some extent, and I think I know that those two brands of Jews were really twins. They were both born out of the painful marriage between anti-Semitic clichés, Jewish self-hatred, the secret wish to resemble our past tormentors, and indeed out of a certain Zionist wish to adopt both the stereotypic Jew of our enemies and its negative—negative not in the moral sense, but almost in the photographic sense of the word negative.

The Jewish dark hair and pale skin had to turn through the Zionist darkroom into the Sabra's blond hair and dark skin. A *sheigetz* is what my own parents used to call me throughout my childhood, though they would never teach me Yiddish, so that I didn't even know what *sheigetz* meant. I only sensed or felt that *sheigetz* was the most endearing word in their entire endearing vocabulary. When they really wanted to be nice to me, when they were excited about me, or when they were worshiping me, they'd call me *sheigetz*. It took me many years to find out that a *sheigetz* is actually nothing but a little Ukranian peasant boy who herds pigs and throws stones at Jews. Why should my parents, the offspring of rabbis and scholars, wish for their offspring in his turn to be a *sheigetz*? They were, by the way, both dark-haired; and through an unprecedented genetic effort they have begotten me blond. If there ever was a tragic, unnecessary triumph, it was in their begetting me blond.

So yes, there is a certain subterranean struggle going on still, to this very day, between the new Jew and the old Jew between Diaspora and Israel. There is a contest.

Israel, I suspect, I never know—I just sense it—evokes a perpetual mixture of feelings among Diaspora Jews: pride and shame and guilt and security and worrying and embarrassment and kinship and anger and whatnot. Diaspora, for its part, evokes in us Israelis a perpetual mixture of feelings not dissimilar to the mixture of feelings that typifies the attitudes of Diaspora Jews toward Israel.

And yes, there is a certain subterranean struggle. If Israel becomes as attractive, as fascinating, as creative, as wonderful as her dreamers hoped for her to be, then she will be draining your sons and daughters and summoning them and taking them away from their parents. If not, then this particular Diaspora is very likely to become extremely attractive, as it is becoming extremely attractive to our own sons and daughters and draining us.

And, yes, there is always the unthinkable—the subterranean fear that if, yes, worst comes to worst, the unthinkable, and Israel is destroyed . . . this time American Jewry would not fail the test: given a second chance, it would pass the test that it failed during the Hitler years. There would be an enormous airlift, a rescue, and when you people will be wrapping us with blankets and giving us the first, hot glass of milk in the refugee camps in New Jersey, you probably would find it difficult, some of you would, to contain yourself from saying, "Haven't we always warned you?"

The Israelis have a similar, unspoken thought: if the unthinkable happens in this country and anti-Semitism becomes unbearable—a doomsday scenario for American Jews—then, of course, Israeli airborne commandos, on an Entebbe-style raid, would take over the fifteen major airports in America and immediately after blowing up the headquarters of the new anti-Semitic movement in America, airlift the entire American Jewry in one night to refugee camps near Herzliya. And when we people wrap you in blankets and serve you the first hot cup of milk, we won't contain ourselves from telling you, "Haven't we always warned you that this would happen?"

Now this is not a bed of roses. This is an uneasy relationship for all the kinship that is involved, for all the mutual attraction, for all the interdependency. It entails a certain argument. From various Diaspora Jewish spokesmen ranging all the way from George Steiner to Jacob Nuesner, we Israelis hear now and then that the very creation of Israel might have been a mistake—at least an embarrassment. In a word, Diaspora ideology rides again.

George Steiner goes even further by saying that a national state per se is a vain, childish, anachronistic, and dangerous concept. We should aspire to "Judaifying" the entire world by turning it into the arena of one hundred different civilizations, rather than a single nation state. The Jews, says Steiner, whether out of necessity or of their own volition, had presented a universal model of nonterritorial civilization until you Zionists chose to join that nationalistic, nineteenth-century regression. A Jew owning a nation-state, says George Steiner, is like an old man in a kindergarten full of lethal toys. This argument is accompanied by an aggressive accusation: What have you Israelis done to the Jewish genius? What have you produced, contributed to world culture except for a handful of colonels and tank drivers? Just compare this with the richness of Jewish creation in the Diaspora. We Diaspora Jews are the pioneers of culture in almost every sphere. You Israelis are not even New Zealand; just a little, levantine country mired in endless fighting, a source of trouble and embarrassment for everybody—Jew, Arab, and the rest of the world.

We Jews, say the new Diaspora ideologists, have a special universal mission: To be the vitamin of Western civilization, and vitamins are supposed to be scattered, not concentrated. This argument is always decorated with the usual panel, which these spokespersons proudly display: Maimonides, Spinoza, Marx, Freud, Kafka, Einstein, Saul Bellow, the physicists, the mathematicians . . . and it's probably only out of modesty that they don't add their own names to the panel. What can you Zionists present as your contribution? Colonels, peasants, and tank drivers. Big deal.

I am very sorry to have to admit that the usual Zionist reply to this is fairly miserable. We hasten to accuse our rivals of careerism, materialism, cowardice. Sometimes some of our spokesmen sink so low as to use anti-Semitic clichés in this argument. When we feel really cornered we even predict and wish a little pogrom on them. The big, bad goy will come and hit you and then your eyes will open to see our light.

For their part, Diaspora ideologists shell us with their trite paradox: Israel meant to give security to the Jews, to provide them with a safe shelter, but, aha! Israel is the least safe place for the Jew nowadays.

I shall not use the usual defensive and defeatist Zionist answer, namely that Stanford University's marvelous but the Weizmann Institute isn't bad either. Saul Bellow is a great fellow, but Yehuda Amichai is also something. No. Let's move right into the heart of the dispute.

Security. I want to get this one out of the way first. No country in the world enjoys total security. Even Belgium is arming itself with tanks and jet fighters. But the major difference between the Israeli condition and the Jewish condition is the fact that we Israelis are in a position, at least up to a point, to mess up our own destiny. A Jew in Detroit might feel more secure physically than a Jew in Jerusalem (I think he would be wrong, but he might). But it is a security granted to the Jew by others. Israel is not fireproof; but if, Heaven forbid! worst comes to worst and there would be a catastrophe in Israel, it would not be caused by Cossacks or Polish anti-Semites or the Tsar Nicholas or the Nazis. A catastrophe in Israel might be caused by ourselves out of folly, arrogance, or short-sightedness. And we are not short of any of those, unfortunately. But part of our freedom, which we Israeli Jews enjoy and Diaspora Jews do not, is the freedom to avoid catastrophe or to head right into it.

Let us turn now to the more humiliating assault on Israel by the anti-Zionists: creativity, cultural contribution, Marx, Freud, Einstein, Kafka. I have always maintained that a civilization can theoretically exist in one of two modes, either as a museum or as live drama. In a museum, culture, religion, folklore, values, and inheritance are neatly arranged in glass cases and parents take their children to show them those assets and try to inspire them, hoping eventually to hand over the keys of the museum to the next generation so that they in turn will bring more visitors.

This in my view, is a dead end. In the last analysis, a graveyard. Because where there is a museum, even a pretty one, there is no action—no live drama. Their young generation is bound to escape into fresh arenas. New Left, Jews for Jesus, Moonies, you name it. The only advantage of a museum culture is that it is change-proof and corruption-proof. It doesn't cause terrible things. It is not likely to degenerate and lose its human face. In this respect, it is as safe as death itself.

Now, my point is that in all exiles, including America, Jewish culture is essentially in danger of becoming a museum where the only proposition that parents can make to their children is, Please do not assimilate. Please go on running the show—the museum. Please be impressed by the richness of our inheritance.

The other option, as I said, is live drama. And live drama is no rose garden, nor is it ever pure. It is a perpetual struggle; sound and fury. Sometimes even bloodshed. But Israel is the only place in the Jewish world now, where there is a live drama on a large scale at work.

Just how creative and significant is the cultural contribution of Israel? If I may distinguish now between museum civilization and live drama and then distinguish between individual creativity and collective creativity, I would say that in terms of individual creativity, the Diasporas are obviously way ahead of Israel. More celebrities, more Nobel prize winners, better writers, deeper thinkers, I presume. This is only natural. The numbers are not on our side, time is not on our side. The Diaspora has existed for millennia, but we have only been there for four troubled decades; six, seven, eight troubled decades.

But if we turn to collective creations I think Israel has the lead. I shall go so far as to make the chauvinistic claim that since the destruction of East- and Central-European Jewry, the only collective Jewish creation on a remarkable scale takes place in Israel and nowhere else.

I am not suggesting the Jewish exiles never had periods of collective creativity. There were at least three points in time when Jewish Diasporas produced magnificent collective creations: In Babylonia, in medieval Spain, and recently in Eastern Europe. By the way, it may be ironical to point out that the very last major creation of East-European Jewry before its final destruction was Zionism itself.

Collective creation is, of course, not the kind of thing for which someone is likely to get the Nobel prize. But it is the crucial, fertile ground for the great individual creator of the future, and I shall immediately return to this point.

To give you but one example of collective creation: the revival of the modern Hebrew language. Despite the common myth, the revival of Hebrew was not the one-man show of Eliezer Ben Yehuda. It is a magnificent collective creation of the Jews in Israel, and before that, of the Zionists in Eastern Europe. No one is likely to get the Nobel prize for reviving the Hebrew language, but in terms of its contribution to civilization, it may be no less important than the complete works of Saul Bellow, with all due respect to the Nobel Prize Committee.

It is remarkable. To me, the revival of Hebrew began with the first boy who said to the first girl, "I love you," in Hebrew . . . probably in Palestine, probably in Jerusalem, probably in 1899, or 1900, or 1901, around that time. That is when Hebrew had to become intimate not as a result of ideology but as a result of the encounter between Sepharadi and Ashkenazi who had no other common language. It was a Sepharadi boy saying to an Ashkenazi girl, or vice-versa, *"ani ohev otach"* in Hebrew, and that is the moment the language was really revived. Forty years later, when I was a kid, the overall number of speakers of modern Hebrew, worldwide, was about four hundred and fifty thousand . . . most of them in Israel itself, in Palestine. The grown-up population of the country, anybody above fifty, would still speak Yiddish. By now we have about 5.5, perhaps 6 million speakers of Hebrew; 4.5 million in Israel proper, at least 1 million in the occupied territories, and another million, perhaps, in the Diaspora. Remarkable figure, 6 million. Remarkable in many ways, not only because of its immediate connotations, but also because the number of speakers of Hebrew now is larger than the number of speakers of Norwegian. In fact, it is larger than the overall number of English speakers in the days of William Shakespeare (by which I'm not implying that every contemporary Israeli writer is a William Shakespeare. We don't have more than half a dozen of those in Tel Aviv right now.) I could bring one or two other examples of collective creation, but I think the point is clear enough. I do not want, by the way, to idealize the collective creations of Israel. Unlike museums, all my examples, or every example of a collective creation that I can think of is exposed to an immediate threat of corruption and degeneration. It is not by accident that I regard defending the language from degeneration as one of my most immediate tasks. But that is exactly what live drama is all about. The struggle is precisely because we are not a museum.

Now, a George Steiner is entitled to view our collective creations in Israel with sardonic condescension. He is entitled to say ironically, "What's the big deal? What are you waving at us? Is it anything like monotheism, Babylonian Talmud, or Hassidism, which are also collective creations of the Jews in the Diaspora?" Fair enough, as long as the anti-Zionists admit that although we may be a fourth-rate theater and they first-rate critics, nonetheless we are the theater, they the critics. Israel is the Jewish stage of this time, collectively speaking. The Diaspora is the auditorium.

And I am not happy about what is happening on the stage or in the auditorium, historically.

My next point—last but one—is that individual creation in the present Diaspora, or individual creators in the present Diaspora, are living on an overdraft drawing from the nonexistent bank of Jewish Eastern Europe still to this day. Bellow, Malamud, Roth, present company not excluded—perhaps George Steiner himself— even Kafka, would not be who they are were it not for Eastern Europe.

Kafka is an interesting example. There is a fascinating, biographical fact, perhaps an apocryphal story, that toward the end of his life Kafka had not only tried to learn Hebrew but even considered making aliyah and inquired about becoming a kibbutznik. Just imagine, Franz Kafka transformed into Ephraim Kafri, the treasurer of Kibbutz Beit Alpha. That would have been a metamorphosis! Now Kafka, of course, had never set foot in a shtetl in Poland, Galicia, or the Ukraine; yet he is what he is precisely because of the cultural influence of Eastern Europe. To be more specific, he was what he was indirectly thanks to the Kabbala and Hassidism. As a young man he was exposed to some performances of a Yiddish theater company that came to Prague from Poland. He himself described that experience in his diaries as a formative one. It must have been a third-rate Yiddish theater with folklore, mysticism, ghosts, exorcism, miracles; probably the usual Yiddish combination of strict mimetic realism and metaphysical fantasy. But then this is precisely the combination that Kafka in his writings refined and elevated to a masterpiece by redeeming it from its vulgar aspects.

Now suppose a new Kafka is growing up right now, here in San Francisco, California. Suppose he is fourteen years old right now. Let's call him Chuck Bernstein. Let's assume that he is every bit of a genius as Kafka was in his time. His future must, as I see it, depend on an uncle in Jerusalem or an experience by the Dead Sea, or a cousin in a kibbutz or something inspired by the Israeli live drama. Otherwise, with the exception of the possibility that he is growing among the ultra-Orthodox, he will be an American writer of Jewish origin—not a Jewish American writer. He may become a new Faulkner, but not a new Kafka.

In other words, I am suggesting that even individual creation in the future, to the extent that it is going to be Jewish, will depend on Israel to some extent. This is not the end of the world, by the way. As I maintain that in the long run individual creation springs from the fertile ground of collective creation, and as I maintain that perhaps there is no collective creation in the present Diaspora, the only choice for Jews is either to turn to Israel or maybe despair.

Now what do I mean by turn to Israel? My best offer is, of course, mount the stage, steal the show—to the extent that you don't like the show change it right away—steal the show in everything. First and foremost in religion; it is high time that you steal the show in religion in Israel and change it. Steal the show in politics, if you don't like Israeli politics. Steal it in literature, though I'm not that keen for you to steal the show in literature. But let it be. Whoever maintains that the Israeli theater is bad, or that the actors are poor, or that the text is miserable, let him or her join and steal the show.

As a second best, whoever does not want or cannot mount the stage—and who am I to preach?—at least learn Hebrew so that you can follow the drama without earphones. If you don't do even that, at least try to move toward the front rows of the auditorium. And if even this is too much for you, and I'm now paraphrasing an old Hassidic tale, the very least you can do is turn your seats in the right direction.

If you have decided, or you feel doomed to be cut off from the stage, removed from the language, the only collective Jewish language of our times, for better or worse, far from the action (good or bad), at least recognize where the action is.

I do not think that having said this I cast a verdict on the future of Diaspora. Certainly I don't think it's my business to preach to you to make aliyah; I'm not in the business of inflicting guilty feelings. Rather I would say, I am in the seduction squad. But I do think that recognizing the centrality of Israel, not necessarily the excellency of Israel but the centrality of Israel, is crucial and vital for your own collective future, if indeed you want to avoid the option or the danger of becoming a spectacularly beautiful museum but, in the long run, Heaven forbid!, an empty one. I don't wish this on you; I am worried. And I thought I should share my worries with you.

# Imagining the Other: 2

## Cynthia Ozick

I hope you will be sympathetic to a very great difficulty. Although I am listed on the program as "respondent," I, like you, have just heard the remarkably stimulating comments of these distinguished gentlemen for the very first time. It's true that our moderator, before I came out to California, gave me, on the telephone, a one-sentence notion of *his* notion of what each previous speaker would say. So it's my early notion of the moderator's early notion of what was *maybe* going to be said here that I will be responding to.

But even on the basis of that uncertain, shorthand, thumbnail telephone impression, I already knew that I was going to be not so much a "respondent" as a dissenter. And as long as it seemed I wasn't going to agree anyhow, I took the considerable risk of writing down a few musings in advance. So if the following paragraphs seem to be only partly or even eccentrically applicable to what has gone before, I hope you will understand my predicament.

I believe there is an unseen guest, or ghost, in this auditorium tonight. Who is it that lurks and stalks among us, leaving his recognizable ideational trail (even when, as we have seen, that trail is being denied)? It is, I think the cultural maven George Steiner (and it's a proof of the organic unity of the Jewish mind that without knowing what Leon Wieseltier and Amos Oz would say, I too have been drawn to speak of George Steiner!)—but surely Steiner's sensibility is present here, whether as precursor, or reflection, or independent inventor, I know not. And it doesn't matter. What matters is that the ideas we have just heard have their currency, even their fame. Not that they are by any means majoritarian or popular views—far from it! It's only that ideas about culture often enough appear to be born out of the egg of the Zeitgeist—as if they are dictated by the very air we breathe. It's engaging to notice that George Steiner too sees America as far, far from centrality, as a great museum or warehouse. George Steiner too defends marginality and homelessness. "Yes," he has written, "I *am* a wanderer, a

*Luftmensch.* . . . But I have made of my harrying . . . a creative impulse so strong that it has recast much of the politics, art and intellectual constructs of the age." Far from being cultural disaster, outsideness becomes cultural opportunity. "Marx lies in Highgate and Freud in Golders Green . . . Einstein's ashes were scattered off New Jersey." Think also of Trotsky, Kafka, Levi-Strauss, Spinoza, Heine. When you declare yourself not quite at home within a society, you are also claiming the possibility of larger and more fertile perspectives. You are pronouncing yourself, as Steiner does, "unto the elements . . . free." Or as Leon puts it, "A Jew may not be able to live happily unless he lives doubly. Why must a whole be found?" As for America as a museum, Steiner is fairly ferocious. It isn't his concern, of course, to posit America as a Jewish museum, as beyond the possibility of fresh Jewish cultural force; Steiner's view is that America is a warehouse for *all* of Western achievement—which would include much of Jewish achievement. The "summits" in literature, in music, in painting, in philosophy and social thought, he charges, all derive from Europe. For instance, when an American theater presents an opera, it is offering itself as a museum of European musical expression. "The pressure," Steiner writes, "of presence throughout the world of the mind and moral feeling exercised on civilization by a Marx, a Freud, even a Levi-Strauss, is of a caliber which American culture does not produce."

Now obviously what we have heard from Amos and Leon is different in nuance and emphasis and direction from Steiner's ideas, and in all respects Jewishly richer. But in all cases the focus is on culture—its priority of location, its expression, how it travels, what it consists of, what it welcomes, what it resists. Culture, after all, is what a society invents, how a society adapts. And it goes without saying that each society lives out its own culture. But does it also go without saying that separated communities of Jews will, through the natural process of living out differing cultures, end up in the position of having to "imagine the Other?"

And right here, right at the very start, just looking at the rubric under which we have been asked to speak tonight, I feel the full roar of dissent. Imagining the Other? I want to protest the phrase itself—for its overuse and therefore its uselessness, for its staleness and paleness, for its throttling of the very thing it asks us to be cognizant of: the imagination. To imagine a Jew who lives across the ocean in another country, speaking another language—to imagine such a Jew as the Other requires small imagination indeed. That sort of imagining belongs to the sociologists, a word I intend to use pejoratively. I speak English, you speak Hebrew, so you are the Other. I have one set of social habits or mores, you have a different set, so you are the Other. I live in a country at peace, you live in a country at war, so you are the Other—as if Israel under threat would not more than anything else draw Jews together! I vote in one kind of democratic elective process, you vote in another kind, so you are the Other. What kind of imagining is this, and who could possibly be interested in it? Or moved by it? Even when you complicate it, even when you try to enrich it, it can't carry us very far. Let us say that the Jews of Israel and the Jews of North America are beginning to develop two crucially separate histories, based on all the differences we already know, and on some still more crucial differences that the future may bring and will surely bring: how does *that* affect imagination? Well, not very much. It isn't the concrete progression of history that matters so much—it isn't the social stuff of *event* that matters so much—as historical consciousness. Two separate histories—the history of the Jews in Iraq, for example, and the history of the Jews in Minsk—are less influenced by their societal and cultural separateness than they are influenced by the principle of their conceptual unity.

Cultural imagination, it seems to me, is a diminishing thing, an impoverishing thing, above all a transient and gossamer thing: an ad hoc thing, a temporary and contemporary contrivance, readily obsolescent, like a horseshoe or videotape—hardly appropriate for what we like to honor by the name of Imagination. For Jews, it isn't culture that belongs to the work of the Imagination; it's the substratum beneath culture. And the work of the Imagination, the work of the substratum, is the work of one's grandmother's knee. It was at my grandmother's knee, and nowhere else—certainly not from George Steiner!—that I learned that, among Jews, there *is* no Other, whatever geographical or biographical or cultural differences and separations might obtain. And if the Jews are to be put to the task of imagining, it ought to be to claim the deepest, the most recalcitrant, the most rewarding, the most treasured, the most lasting, the most fundamental and essential substratum. Not the operatics and vagaries and moods and movements of culture, but the reason *for* culture. Not the sociology or mores of culture, but the motives of culture.

The imagination of the substratum is similar to the imagination of novelists and original essayists, though not quite—because novelists and essayists speak in the language of modernism, and for the substratum, modernism is simply another bauble, another current of the short run. Still, the novelistic imagination slices through expectations grounded in historical event, and it is the diminished imagination of empiricists, sociologists, and cultural pragmatists—and this includes many critics and historians—that sticks with expectations grounded in historical event. "If thus and thus is the case, then thus and thus will result" is the whole reach of such thinking. But the social approach of history is not enough; it cannot penetrate to the substratum. In the language of modernism, culture is and has always been a Jewish pursuit because it is engaged in vigorous categorizing, in the robust drawing of distinctions. That's why, when George Steiner names his great names among those who exert "mind and moral feeling" on civilization, it is no surprise that he names Jews—Jews who have invented new categories and dreamed of fresh distinctions never before observed in the world of run-of-the-mill expectation. It's a thing agreeable to the Jewish brain to know that one thing is not another thing, to avoid blurring, to know that *milchig* is not *fleishig,* God is not man, and so on. The making of distinctions is a significant intellectual act, and it is of course the work of culture. But it is not the work of the imagination of the substratum.

We call ourselves Jews, we think of ourselves as one people, but not because of culture. After a while—and not a very long while, either—culture divides. Language especially divides, because language is the preeminent vessel and vehicle of culture. Yehuda Amichai, writing a poem about Jews in Jerusalem, and writing it in Hebrew, knows something that Harvey Shapiro, writing a poem about Jews in New York, and writing it in English, doesn't know; and vice versa. A Jewish political leftist or a Jewish political conservative in Tel Aviv is nowadays notably different from a Jewish political leftist or a Jewish political conservative in New York. (Incidentally—and parenthetically—I received, just before leaving New York, a telegram from Israel, signed "Israwriters." It said: "Please protest delegating 15 leftist writers for Berkeley symposium excluding all others." So it may even turn out that Left and Right in the same polity are developing into separate, unmixable societies.) One could go on and on enumerating the nuances and tendrils of social, historical, and biographical differentiation that occur among bodies of Jews who live apart from one another in evolving communities.

But the imagination of the substratum—that visionary and unifying space and utterance beneath culture—asks for something else. It asks for the underlying magma, the organic plasm, that seizes all of us—wherever we live, and however we live, and whatever our ideology, and whatever our mores-system—and allows us to call ourselves Jews. Some will want to name this underlying space and utterance Jewish destiny; I am not among them. If destiny includes what other people have done or will do to you, then destiny is of little interest. What is of interest is what one fashions and invents for oneself, out of one's own substance and conscience and imagination. For others the substratum is, simply and crudely, "Jewish religion"; I am certainly not among these. "Religion," it seems to me, is a coarse and even cartoonlike word, a Roman word, foreign to Jewish thought and sensibility.

What, then, *is* the imagination of the substratum, this flexible tissue that unites all Jews, erasing the alienating notion of the Other? That allows Jews to own a single history, however different in factual detail their varying histories may be? That allows me to know—and this is precisely what I learned at my grandmother's knee—that what happened to Jews in Spain happened to me, that what happened to Jews during the First Crusade happened to me, that though my parents came from Minsk I belong to the Jews of Yemen, and they to me, that, though I may live in New York, Jerusalem is mine; that, in that sublime metaphorical formulation the tradition supplies, every Jew in every generation stood together at Sinai; and that therefore every Jewish culture is my culture, *especially* when it is what Amos calls "collective culture"? And that there is not, there never will be, a Jewish Other?

I am not going to undertake, in this brevity, to denote what the Jewish substratum is, or to attempt to describe it. This is not to say that it cannot be described, or that we ought to avoid describing it. That it has something to do, indispensably, with the nature of the imagination that gave birth to the strenuous idea of monotheism is vital. That it has something to do, indispensably, with the rejection of idolatry of every kind is also vital. Leon, we have heard, in his assault on anything even faintly touching on the metaphysical, calls the substratum a "romantic unity toward an epiphanous end." And indeed it may be the substratum that Amos Elon speaks of when he refers scathingly to "metahistorical phenomena." But it is important to see how the penetrating imagination that can drill into the substratum, while its force is metaphysical, does not shut out the secularists, agnostics, or even the self-declared atheists among us. In fact it defines them, it forms them, it creates them.

So I won't accept this fragment, this partial sighting, this insufficiency, this indigestible truism called "the Other." As long as I strive to be connected to the substratum, I cannot be said to live in a museum. A museum is a passive receptacle. Connecting with the substratum requires rigor and alertness, and the rejection of easy belief; it requires a historic capability more courageous than politics and topicality; it requires a profundity of originality— meaning a sense of the *origin* of things. The Diaspora—the idea of a cultural museum—is located wherever Jews become careless and neglectful of the substratum, and are content to settle for cultural criticism only, however rich and alluring and fascinatingly catego- rized that cultural criticism may be. This means that the Diaspora has the insidious capacity to spread everywhere, and can be found in Jerusalem, Haifa, and Tel Aviv, as well as Toronto, Chicago and San Francisco. Jerusalem is not a cultural capital in the way of Paris or New York. Jerusalem cannot be rated by the number of internationally famous writers it turns out, though it does that sort of thing very nicely too. The measure of the value of the flesh-and- blood earthly Jerusalem is how good it can be at annihilating the creeping, distracting, draining notion, the damning and dooming notion, of Otherness among Jews. The rabbis remind us that what destroyed the Temple was not foreign invasion, but groundless divi- sion. Amos: Israel belongs to all Jews wherever they are, and the show (to seize your image) is already stolen.

# The Politics of Translation: Amichai and Ravikovitch in English

## Chana Bloch

Some lines in a love poem of Yehuda Amichai's, "A Precise Woman," illustrate very neatly a problem all translators grapple with, that of literal vs. "free" translation. Amichai writes in praise of his beloved:

> *Afilu tsa'akot ha-ta'avah lefi seder,*
> *ahat aharey ha-shniya ve-lo me'urbavot:*
> *yonat bayit, ahar kakh yonat bar,*
> *ahar kakh tavas, tavas patsua, tavas, tavas.*
> *Ahar kakh yonat bar, yonat bayit, yona yona*
> *tinshemet, tinshemet, tinshemet.*

> Even her cries of passion follow a certain order,
> one after the other:
> tame pigeon, then wild pigeon,
> then peacock, wounded peacock, screeching peacock,
> then wild pigeon, tame pigeon, pigeon pigeon
> thrush, thrush, thrush.

The word I've translated as "thrush" is *tinshemet* in Hebrew; its current dictionary definition is "barn owl, barn owl, barn owl." What is one to do? I lifted mine eyes unto the Bible, whence help often comes. But *tinshemet* appears only three times in the Bible, and no one seems to know what it means. In Lev. 11:18 (and Deut. 14:16), the *tinshemet,* along with the vulture and the bat, is listed among the unclean birds that we are prohibited from eating; in the Bibles I consulted, it is translated variously as "swan" (AV), "water hen" (RSV), and "little owl" (NEB). To add to the confusion, a little later in the same chapter of Leviticus (11:30), the *tinshemet* appears in a list of unclean creeping things; here I found it translated as "mole" (AV) and "chameleon" (RSV, NEB).

When I turned back to the Hebrew, it struck me that Amichai

130

was not thinking of any of these "abominations" (though a case could be made for that large-eyed night bird, the owl). I asked him whether he chose *tinshemet* primarily for its sound, and he confirmed my guess. *Tinshemet* is based on the verbal root *nasham*, "to breathe," and in this context, the sibilant *sh* suggests breathing—or heavy breathing, I should say. So I found "thrush," perched between albatross and zebra finch in my trusty thesaurus. But since I'm a little shaky on the names of birds—I know a hawk from a handsaw and an owl from a pussycat, that's about it—I was relieved to see that Webster's identifies the thrush as a European bird, which brings it within Amichai's purview. Then I discovered, in his "Seven Laments for the War Dead," that Amichai once read about the thrush in an old German zoology text. And so it came to pass that the lady recovers from her passion—in English—like a thrush.

This example illustrates the point that in translation it is often the spirit of the word, not the letter, that is called for. It also suggests that a "free" translation is not always the result of an unfettered flight of the imagination. You open the Bible (or rather, the Bibles), the concordance, the dictionary, the thesaurus, the complete works of the poet—and let your fingers do the walking. Then you can fly.

A problem all translators of Hebrew poetry must confront is that of biblical allusion. Israeli readers, who are required to study the Bible, even in the secular public schools, from their earliest years, have no trouble with such allusions. There is clearly a difficulty, however, in English. I am reminded of the discussions about staging Pyramus and Thisby in *Midsummer Night's Dream:* how do you bring in the Bible without frighting the ladies? Bottom and his friends come up with two kinds of solutions. Starveling, on the one hand, recommends cutting whatever is likely to be troublesome; Bottom, on the other, plumps for elaboration and explanation. "Write me a prologue," he begs.

A translator of Hebrew poetry often faces these two choices. Let me offer you an example of each. The first comes from Amichai's "Seven Laments for the War Dead":

> *Adon Beringer, she-bno*
> *nafal ba-te'alah, hafaruha*
> *zarim bishvil oniyot, la'avor ba-midbar,*
> *over derekh sha'ar yafo, leyadi.*

> Mr. Beringer, whose son
> fell at the Canal that strangers dug

> so ships could cross the desert,
> crosses my path at Jaffa Gate.

In the second line and third lines, *nafal ba-te'alah hafaruha zarim,*
Amichai echoes one of the oldest poems in the Bible, the "Song
of the Well" from the Book of Numbers:

> *Ali be'er enu lah:*
> *be'er hafaruha sarim.*
>
> Spring up, o well; sing ye into it:
> The princes digged the well.
>
> (Num. 21:17–18, AV)

This biblical verse is familiar to Israelis, first of all because they
have to study it—perhaps to memorize it—in school. They are even
more likely to know a version of it in the popular folk dance-and-
song, *be'er ba-sadeh hafaruha ro'im* (in this case, it's a "well dug
by shepherds"). The biblical poem about digging a well in the de-
sert and the hopeful song from Israel's pioneer days are both heard
in Amichai's line about the Suez Canal, the scene of deadly battles
in the Yom Kippur war; they serve to intensify, by contrast, the
poet's sorrow for the fallen soldier. Encountering a biblical allusion
of this sort in Hebrew, the reader becomes an archaeologist, tunnel-
ing down and discovering older and older strata right beneath his
feet.

Much as I admire this line, I must admit it's the sort of thing
that can drive a translator to distraction. Suppose I were to mimic
the archaism, echoing the language of the AV, and say Mr. Be-
ringer's son "fell at the Canal that strangers *digged*": what exactly
would I achieve? No readers would understand why I availed myself of the King's English unless they already knew the Hebrew
verse. They certainly wouldn't have the exquisite literary pleasure
of hearing three different texts resound together, as they do in
Amichai's poem. All they would gain is a threepenny archaism to
prove that the translator did her homework. If they were attentive
readers, they might even wonder if the translator made some mistake. In a case like this, to paraphrase Bottom's friend, "I believe
we must leave the allusion out, when all is done."

On the other hand, there are times when the translator needs to
elaborate, to "write a prologue" of sorts, in order to bring the
allusion home to the reader. One of Dahlia Ravikovitch's recent
poems is about an unknown man who was shot in the Hebron
marketplace and left to die because no one knew his identity; the

Jews assumed he was an Arab, and the Arabs, a Jew. The last stanza reads:

> Ki yimatse halal ba-sade,
> ki yimatse halal ba-adama,
> ve-yat'su zekenekha ve-shahatu egla
> ve-et efra ba-nahal yefazru.

> If a dead body is found lying in the field,
> if a body is found in the open,
> let your elders go out and slaughter a heifer
> and scatter its ashes in the river.

These lines are based on Deut. 21:1–9; without reference to the Bible, their point would probably be lost on many readers. Exactly how much help does the reader need in confronting a biblical allusion? A footnote didn't seem quite enough in this instance. Crucial to the meaning of the poem, though not explicitly mentioned, are some lines at the end of the biblical passage:

And all the elders . . . shall wash their hands over the heifer. . . . And they shall . . . say, Our hands have not shed this blood, neither have our eyes seen it. . . . And the blood shall be forgiven them. (Deut. 21:6–9)

When Ariel Bloch and I translated this poem, we decided not only to name the passage in question but also to quote from it at some length. Then we moved the quotation from the notes at the end of the book and set it as an epigraph to the poem. Finally, we talked about changing the poem's title. The educated reader of Hebrew would recognize the title, "Egla Arufa," as biblical, and would know that Ravikovitch is writing about the community's response to the loss of a human life, about guilt and collective responsibility and ritual absolution. A literal translation into English, "Beheaded Heifer," has no such implications. Casting about for a title that would have something like the same resonance, we considered taking a phrase from the biblical verse I've just quoted: "Our Hands Have Not Shed This Blood." This phrase points up—perhaps too insistently?—the question of our communal willingness to come to terms with our responsibility. We also thought of "Scattering Ashes," from the last line of the poem, which suggests a familiar ritual for laying the dead to rest. We finally settled on "Blood Heifer" because it summons up the archaic ritual of the

Hebrew title, and thus underscores, by contrast, our community's painful confusion.

I have been talking about what it means to uproot a poem from its homeland and send it into exile. "How shall we sing the Lord's song in a strange land?" Not every poem is able to make a new life for itself under such conditions.

Let me offer an example from Yiddish. A few years ago I was asked to translate some poems by Abraham Sutzkever for *The Penguin Book of Modern Yiddish Verse*. On the list of poems assigned to me was *Di Blayene Platn fun Roms Drukeray* ("The Lead Plates at the Rom Press"), which Sutzkever wrote in September 1943 in the Vilna Ghetto. The Rom Press was one of the great Jewish publishing houses of Eastern Europe, famous for its editions of the Talmud as well as of modern Yiddish and Hebrew literature. Sutzkever's poem is based on the Jewish underground's plans to melt down the lead printing plates of the Rom Press and turn them into ammunition. The first stanza sounds like this:

> *Mir hobn vi finger geshtrekte durkh gratn*
> *zu fangn di likhtike luft fun der fray—*
> *durkh nakht zikh getsoygn, tzu nemen di platn,*
> *di blayene platn fun Roms Drukeray.*
> *Mir, troymer, badarfen itst vern soldatn*
> *un shmeltsen oyf koyln dem gayst funem blay.*

The subject of the poem may be summarized in the last two lines of this stanza: "We dreamers must now become soldiers / and smelt into bullets the spirit of the lead."

I was reluctant to undertake this translation, not only because of the declamatory tone, which doesn't travel easily, but also because of the rhythm, which is very regular, very emphatic in Yiddish; the poem asks to be set to march music. Since Sutzkever is a master of prosody who delights in subtle effects, we can assume he has deliberately chosen this drumbeat regularity. The great temptation for a translator is to make the rhythm more subtle, that is, more palatable to the reader of English. But if you use slant rhyme and tone down the march-rhythms, you misrepresent the original. On the other hand, if you faithfully reproduce the thumping rhythms, the reader will more than likely assume you've done a poor job of translation. You can hardly add a footnote saying, "Dear Reader, the rhythm is like that in Yiddish, too. Sutzkever did it on purpose. I did it on purpose." This is a no-win situation for a translator. There's no way to be true to the original and, at the same time, to make a poem that doesn't sound clumsy in English.

I had an exchange of letters about this poem with Ruth Wisse, one of the editors of the volume, along with Irving Howe and Khone Shmeruk. Ruth's argument almost convinced me:

> Sutzkever became a folk hero in the ghetto for reasons that had nothing to do with subtleties, though the poem is actually far subtler than it appears, despite the rhythm and militant rhyme. [So he ought to be] represented by at least one poem of a hortatory public nature. On the one hand, we want the volume to contain the best poems. On the other, if as finicky a poet as Sutzkever modified his idea of poetry to this degree for these reasons, can we falsify the record with only nature, Israeli landscape, ruminations, exotica, aesthetic credo?

As an editor, of course, Ruth was perfectly right in wanting to include the poem. But as a translator, I didn't feel equal to the task. I wrote back to say, "Please find someone else." But not without a twinge of guilt. I asked myself: Does my responsibility to the vanished culture require that I make the attempt? Do I have the luxury of aesthetic choice?

Recently I found myself on the other side of the fence—or to be more exact, on both sides of it. Ariel Bloch and I just translated and edited a collection of Dahlia Ravikovitch's, *The Window: New and Selected Poems,* drawing upon five volumes of poetry published between 1959 and 1986. In the 1986 volume, *Real Love,* there's a section of overtly political poems, under the heading *Sugyot be-Yahadut bat-Zmanenu* ("Issues in Contemporary Judaism"). Ariel and I at first omitted all but one of these poems—on aesthetic grounds, we told ourselves: they seemed to us declamatory and shrill (as is often the case with political poetry), far less complex and subtle than most of Ravikovitch's work. This view was supported by Dahlia herself, who told us in a phone conversation that many of these poems were "newspaper verse." "They were good when they were written, at the time of the war in Lebanon," she said, "but now, six years later, some of them seem outdated, too sharp; they don't all hold up as poems." Finally, she left the editorial decision to us, with the understanding that we would make the decision on aesthetic grounds.

We had decided to include only a token sample of these political poems when, with one strong word, our good friend and colleague Chana Kronfeld made us rethink the whole question. To omit these poems, Chana suggested, would be tantamount to censorship. As it happened, I'd had an experience of censorship in Israel, where

I lived between 1964 and 1967. I'd written a journalistic account
for *Midstream* about my experiences as an American in Jerusalem
in the period just before the 1967 war, and I was told I had to have
it cleared by the censor. This gentleman, wearing his army khakis,
sat behind a little gooseneck lamp and read through my piece as I
stood waiting for his stamp of approval. He paused for a while over
some sentences in which I had written that people were crowding
into the supermarket to stock up on imperishables—sugar, flour,
macaroni, matza, cooking oil. "Now, how will that look in *hutz
l'aretz* [abroad]?" he said, half to himself and half to me. "Won't it
create the wrong impression?" I was caught between conflicting
emotions. As a witness, I was committed to telling the truth, the
*whole* truth; to omit what's disagreeable is a form of lying. At the
same time, I understood his anxiety that the whole truth might in
some way be problematic. That memory came back to me with a
vengeance when I heard the word "censorship."

At the kitchen table, Ariel and I wrestled with the issues. *The
Window,* we told ourselves, is a collection of *New and Selected
Poems;* its purpose is to give the reader a notion of Ravikovitch's
best work. Many readers will be drawn to the political poems because they are so shocking, perhaps to the neglect of the other
poems. We could imagine a reviewer who would fasten on a line
like *Tinok lo horgim pa'amayim,* "You can't kill a baby twice," as
an occasion to talk politics, instead of attending to the body of
Dahlia's work over a period of thirty years.

On the other hand, we told ourselves, these poems represent a
real turning point in Ravikovitch's career as a poet. Much of her
earlier work is about her personal suffering, and has been faulted
for solipsism; in these more recent poems, she brings her sensibility and power of expression to new subjects: the anguish caused
by war, the resemblances between the plight of the Palestinians
and that of the Jews, the moral dilemma of the Israelis. Such a
dramatic turn in her work could not be glossed over without seriously distorting the picture. Precisely because we were putting
together a representative collection, we had an obligation, a responsibility, to include the political poems.

Even the aesthetic argument against these poems wasn't entirely
convincing to us. Granted, we included what we consider to be
Ravikovitch's best work, but clearly some poems in the manuscript
are better than others. Besides, we wondered, aren't the political
poems somewhat more effective than we at first admitted? They
certainly make us feel uncomfortable; isn't that a sign of their

power? And finally, is our standard of judgment really just "aesthetic"? Isn't it colored by some underlying anxiety?

Ay, there's the rub. These poems were written in Hebrew for an Israeli audience that has the competence—the knowledge of the language, as well as of the literary and political context—to make sense of them. To translate them into English is to thrust them into a different milieu, where they may very well be misunderstood, perhaps even misused.

Consider the following lines from a poem called "New Zealand":

> K'var en od ta'am le-hastir:
> anahnu nisayon she-lo ala yafe,
> tokhnit she-nishtabsha,
> krukha be-ratzhanut rabba mi-day.

> No point in hiding it any longer:
> we're an experiment that didn't turn out well,
> a plan that went wrong,
> tied up with too much murderousness.

Given the "sanctity" of the Zionist dream, "an experiment that didn't turn out well" is almost a blasphemy. Here Ravikovitch gives voice to her anger and frustration in Hebrew, in the closed circle of the family, where all angers start. I first heard words like these in Jerusalem, where I lived with my family between 1984 and 1986. What does it mean to send such words out into the world?

There is no doubt that they may be misunderstood. When I quoted this stanza to an American who is a devoted Zionist, he became incensed: "How could Dahlia say the experiment has failed? Why, of all the states established since World War II, Israel is clearly the most successful! And what's this stuff about going off to New Zealand [the ostensible subject of the poem]? Doesn't she know there are race wars in New Zealand?"

We were more troubled, of course, by the anticipated response of readers who are not at all sympathetic to Israel. "Tell it not in Gath, publish it not in the streets of Askelon; lest the daughters of the Philistines rejoice, lest the daughters of the uncircumcised triumph" (2 Sam. 1:20). If we "publish" these poems in the streets of Berkeley and New York, won't some people rejoice, perhaps even triumph? Is that what we want? Is that what Dahlia wanted?

There are some further difficulties in the stanza I have just quoted. The last line here reads krukha be-ratzhanut rabba mi-day. In our literal version of the poem we had first translated the Hebrew

noun *ratzhanut* as "murderousness." But the syllable-counter inside me, the little metrical abacus, got all rattled: "You can't say
'murderousness,' Chana. Too many syllables, too many s's. Try
'savagery.'" Who was the tempter who whispered that? Wasn't I
secretly glad that there were too many syllables, too many s's, so
we'd have to go looking for another word, one we could live with
more easily? But then, is "savagery" really more bearable? And
by how much?

Other possibilities we considered were "too much murder in the
air" and "too much murder on everyone's mind." Both are strong,
though not strong enough. *Ratzhanut* is not just something in the air,
like pollen: the Hebrew word refers to both the mentality and the
action. "Murderousness" sounded odd to me; though I found it in
Webster's and the OED, I wasn't sure I'd ever heard it spoken or
seen it in print. Finally it was the very clumsiness of the word that
appealed to me. Glibness, ease—perhaps those are the real dangers
when we are talking about painful realities. "Murderousness" carries
a certain measure of conviction in its very awkwardness.

There's one final difficulty in this line. What does Ravikovitch
mean by *ratzhanut rabba mi-day,* "too much murderousness"? Is
"too much" simply a loose way of saying "a lot of"? In that case,
should we smooth out the logic in English, in order to prevent
further misunderstanding? Or is she saying, rather, that the very
existence of nation-states inherently involves a certain level of murderousness; that a low level, while not desirable, may be tolerable,
like a low rate of tar and nicotine? We followed the Hebrew phras-
ing exactly, hoping that our readers would come up against that
question on their own.

In one of her recent poems, "Jewish Portrait," Ravikovitch
writes about the Diaspora Jew who "looks around in fear." Was
that, we wondered, our initial response in confronting these political poems? "How will it look to the *goyim?*" was one of the theme
songs of my childhood, as the daughter of Russian Jews in the
Bronx, and of Ariel's, as the son of German Jews in Nahariya.

Our final decision about what to include was in some way influenced by the poems themselves. In the most haunting of Ravikovitch's new poems, "Hovering at a Low Altitude," the speaker
presents herself as a witness to the rape of a young Arab girl,
and describes herself satirically as watching from a distance and
doing nothing:

> *Mahshevotay ripduni birfida shel mokh.*
> *Matsati li shita pshuta me'od,*

*lo midrakh regel ve-lo ma'of.*
*Rehifa be-gova namukh.*

My thoughts cushion me gently, comfortably.
I've found a very simple method,
not with my feet on the ground, and not flying—
hovering
at a low altitude.

"My thoughts cushion me gently, comfortably"—the irony of these lines was painful to us. In deciding which poems to include, we didn't want to "hover at a low altitude"; we didn't want to make a "comfortable" choice. The decision not to be political would have been, after all, a political decision.

# On Reading American Jewish Writers

## Hanoch Bartov

I wish that Americans would have been reading Hebrew writers of
all generations as we have been devoutly reading American literature—Jew, gentile, South, West, New England and what have you.
The first book that I remember having read was an American
novel, *Uncle Tom's Cabin*. The first book ever. And we have read
Upton Sinclair, and Sinclair Lewis, and then Dos Passos, and
Hemingway and then Steinbeck, and then all the long list of American Jewish writers from the very beginning from Ludwig Lewison
up to the last.

I even spent my recent trip from Tel Aviv to New York reading
*Envy,* or *Yiddish in America,* by Cynthia Ozick, one of the greatest
stories I've ever read, Jewish or non-Jewish.

I have learned something from this conference. I did not come
with the hope that we are going to make you into Zionists, and I
am sure that you did not come with the hope that we will come
and join the American Jewish writers. But we have learned a lot.

Let me suggest a synopsis for an American-Israeli novel. I say
it in both an ambivalent and very hopeful vein because it is my
feeling that it is an ongoing thing between us. I do not know what
is going to be in fifty years. I am doubtful, but the last hundred
years were not so bad. This story too begins a hundred years ago,
but I will start it from much later. Three years ago I went to Portland, Oregon, and I had a list handed over to me of people that I
should meet. One of the people that I was supposed to meet was
a lecturer at the university and a rabbi by the name of Joshua
Stampfer. I saw the name and I wondered, Joshua Stampfer, Portland, Oregon? I remembered that there was a Yehoshua Stampfer
a hundred years ago, one of the founders of Petach Tikvah. Being
a book mouse, I remembered that I read a long time ago in a book
about Petach Tikvah that this Stampfer visited America in 1881.
There was one single item in one single Hebrew paper, *haMaggid,*
from July 1881, which reports Stampfer's visit to Chicago. That

140

was after Petach Tikvah had been deserted, for the first time, and he went to America to organize support for rebuilding it. The report ends by saying that: the result of this meeting in Chicago was that such a society was founded and the members pledged a certain annual sum for the support of those who would come to the Holy Land to toil its soil.

Okay. So I come to Portland, Oregon, and see this man. I look at his face, and he is a Stampfer, no question. They are Hungarian Jews; they have a very prominent face and I have known them all. The son of the founder was a mayor of Petakh Tikvah, Reb Shloimeh Stampfer. I look at him and I look at him and I say, "Are you the grandson?"

This was the first thing I said. Not *Shalom,* nothing. "Are you the grandson?" He said, "No, I am the grand-grandson." I ask him, "What do you do in Portland, Oregon?" And then I heard the following story. In 1881 when this first Stampfer went to America he not only went to Chicago, he also went to Salt Lake City, where there was already a Jewish community. While he was in Salt Lake City he took out an American citizenship, and then went back to Petach Tikvah to found modern Palestine with an American passport in his pocket. He never went back to America. Never. And he had sons and grandsons, and one of the sons was the mayor, Reb Shloimeh. One of Reb Shloimeh's sons in 1924, with the new U.S. Immigration Act, where naturalized citizens were about to lose their citizenship if they did not go back to America, took his children and went to Akron, Ohio, to become the rabbi. And he stayed there.

This Yehoshua Stampfer of Portland, Oregon, his son, an American professor and so on, is actually on an American passport taken out when Petach Tikvah was founded more than a century ago.

We have a very complex and ambivalent relationship. To end the story, as Agnon would have said, not on a sour note, this Yehoshua Stampfer has a son; his name is Shaul, Saul, and Shaul Stampfer is a professor of medieval Jewish history in Jerusalem.

So, my friends, this is the story that I propose to you as the subject of an American-Israeli novel.

# Afterword: The Jewish Writer Unmasked

## Nessa Rapoport

My great-aunt Bella, asked how she sustains her spirits in the face of loneliness and old age, answers simply: Poetry. In the middle of the night, when Jerusalem sleeps, she walks back and forth in her room reciting the Yiddish poems that have been her beloved companions since her youth. At such times, she tells me, her brothers and sisters—all dead, one murdered by the Nazis—are summoned: The songs of childhood are in her ears.

My great-aunt was brought up in a house in which her parents, hearing a crash in the next room, would call out, "It's only a thing, only a thing," before they knew what had been broken. When Bella, the youngest, left her beautifully furnished apartment in Warsaw to follow her new husband to impoverished Palestine, her in-laws importuned her father in Canada to intervene. My paternal great-grandfather wrote back: "Better that a daughter of mine should starve in the streets of Eretz Yisrael than live in plenty in the streets of Poland."

\* \* \*

On January 15, 1991, I am drinking coffee with the Israeli writer Meir Shalev at the Laromme Hotel in Jerusalem. We speak of our writing and our children. And we speak of the war, which may be imminent, which may break out tonight. Meir has the familiar Israeli panache; it is business as usual for him. He is writing in his office today and would not even prepare a sealed room against a possible chemical attack if it weren't for a conservative feeling of parental responsibility, he says.

I have my own feeling of responsibility to my son, Joshua, known in Israel as Yehoshua Yair. Like Meir, I have no concern for myself. But I wonder, as Joshua's curly head appears and disappears amidst the café tables, whether I am right in obliging him to participate in Jewish destiny quite so soon. At two and a half, he cannot look at a mask of any kind without shaking in my arms. On the morning of January 15, we are in a country where as early as midnight everyone will likely don a mask, and I, Joshua's mother, will be urging him into a plastic tent, my face distorted, unrecognizable to him.

Outside the hotel, Jerusalem is ravishing. In truth, before my departure from New York I worried more about the weather than the war. Having endured two winters of Jerusalem's unique chill, I vainly wished that my Israeli nephew—whose bar mitzvah was the trip's occasion—had been born in summer.

Jerusalem, however, with the rest of the country, is undergoing a drought. All winter long the traditional prayer book offers language to beseech God that dew and rain fall on this land. As a Zionist I ought to long for rain, but of course I am intoxicated by the translucent light and unnatural balmy air of the city. I am a person of tropical inclination, who loved Israel immediately for the perfume of jasmine and oranges that greeted me on my first arrival, twenty years ago, and for her long Mediterranean summers.

When I behold Jerusalem on this day, I hear old words. "Ten measures of beauty descended upon the world," the Talmud says. "Jerusalem took nine." In the prelude to war, these words are juxtaposed with those of Chaim Nachman Bialik in his poem of pogrom, "In the City of Slaughter." When I look out the window at the unblemished sky, I hear the poet's Hebrew: "The sun shone, the blossom burst—and the slayer slaughtered."

Bialik was crying out against a universe and God that allowed one cruel constancy: Jews can be murdered, and yet the created world proceeds to manifest its beauty, untouched.

On the radio, Galei Tsahal, the army station, is instructing people all day about how to adjust their masks and how to seal their rooms. *"Gemar atimah tovah,"* the announcer ends his hour cheerfully.

It is for my laughter at this pun that my father's father studied Hebrew in Poland, and my mother's parents set aside money so that each grandchild could attend a Jewish dayschool, and my mother keeps a Hebrew novel and dictionary at her bedside, and my father spends his sabbaticals in Israel, where my sister will move within the year. *"Gemar atimah tovah"* or "happy sealing": a phrase parodying the words with which Jews take leave of each other between Rosh Hashanah and Yom Kippur, *"Gemar hatimah tovah"*: "May you be sealed well [in the Book of Life]." For a Jewish writer, this witticism on Israeli radio heralds what we call in our prayers "the beginning of the flowering of our redemption."

I feel quite bohemian and subversive in my embrace of Israel these days. It has now become truly radical to proclaim a faith in Zionism. And yet within forty-eight hours, Israel—unchanged in ideology or practice—will briefly be transformed from anathema/

South Africa into everyone's hero. So much love for being willing to "turn the other cheek," as a British news announcer infelicitously puts it, in language that betrays an even worse acquaintance with the progenitors of Christianity than I expect of the Western world.

*   *   *

It is words that have brought me to this place. The impassioned, resolute voice of my maternal grandmother, who, in an early forties' news commentary on Canada's national radio, said: "Already three million Jews have died; if something is not done, six million will die."

No one is immune from metaphor. The gas masks, sold by Germany to protect Jews against Iraqi gas, fumbled on frantically in sealed rooms: A people that each year recalls its coming out of Egypt 3,500 years ago can certainly remember the archetypes of this century.

And so Bialik's tale and Anne Frank's attic tale inevitably are evoked on this day. But here is another tale, one of renewal and sovereignty that begins to dispel today's anxiety.

In the *Jerusalem Post,* several airlines announce the cancellation of all flights. Others regretfully inform their passengers that due to substantial increases in insurance premiums, a $150 surcharge, payable at the airport, must be imposed. And yet Israel's national airline flies on serenely, taking out Americans and Israelis, should they desire, and bringing home future Israelis from the Soviet Union and Ethiopia.

On January 15, El Al is the emblem of Zionism's success. I feel the triumph of old loyalty; I have always been faithful to El Al. I like the tapes of Israeli music and the Hebrew spoken by the stewards when they think no one is listening. And the way they carry their bodies.

*   *   *

At a time of national crisis, Israeli radio plays the most beautiful songs. They are songs from the records and tapes I have carried back to New York for two decades. I know them all, melodies from before 1948 recorded by contemporary singers. So it is I find myself in a sealed room, breathing shallowly in my mask and waiting for the next scrupulously accurate news report, only to exclaim to anyone within earshot—my husband, his parents, his sister and her husband, their four children, two family friends, and my son in his plastic tent: "I love this song!"

And I do, for in the middle of this Jerusalem night when no one sleeps, I am flung back to another night, a spring night, my first night here, on a journey to my first love, a love framed in the Hebrew of the Song of Songs and a journey when I met not only the boy but also my great-aunt, ardent and full of fortitude.

"We have been through many things before this and will see this through as well," my Israeli friends tell me in Hebrew. I have not been through anything like this, except in my Jewish dreams, for just as every Jew is obliged to see herself as if she, too, stood at Sinai, so every conscious Jew of my generation has imagined herself in such a possible catastrophe.

When my soul cries out in terror, what language does it speak? What if my parents had not bequeathed me this gift, access to the Jewish tongue? Nessa, my son says, confused by my former name, Mommy, his cousins' mother's name, *Ima,* and the urgent "Nessa" that precedes the words of someone who knocks on the door in the middle of the night to be sure we've heard the siren telling us to run upstairs to our sealed room.

I have become an archetype—the Jewish mother of Israel, in whose mythical image everyone from Rachel our foremother to Golda Meir has been described. "Nessa," my son looks up at me and says, "will you take care of me?"

When I come back to New York, how will I tell this? I who have lived for words and by them do not have any language to convey what happens in my body when the insistent siren blares in the Jerusalem night and I wake my sleeping child to race up the stairs.

Two stories are colliding in my head—the North American one that, notwithstanding the Cold War and the Cuban Missile Crisis, was a tale of increasing security, prosperity, and acceptance of me as a Jew; and the older tale, the blood tale, the one I learned first about how in every generation a tyrant arose and who knew from whence our salvation?

Now, in the war, which Jewish body am I, the cossetted Jewish body of my childhood or the vulnerable Jewish body of our historical nightmare?

Classic Zionism tried to redefine the male Jewish body from the pallor of the yeshiva *bocher* bent nearsightedly over his books in the Pale to the bronzed face and bold stance of the *halutz,* looking farsightedly past his ploughed field to a dream of freedom for his people in their own land. A parallel reconstruction of the Jewish woman was not as fully imagined, although we can trace her transformation from a kerchiefed and covered woman in a shtetl to a kerchiefed woman in shorts, the ploughwoman.

We Diaspora Jews who made our first trips to Israel in the early seventies certainly know how Israel changed our bodies: To arrive, as I did then, in April and descend from an airplane into the redolent air, shocking in its potency, was to identify the land forever with youth and sensuality and a tactile freedom undreamed of by our sincere Zionist parents. Has anyone fully described the eros of Israel to the *galut* Jew, the beautiful dark men, the profusion of flowers, the tropical landscape so alien, so ours? Shivering Canadians who lived for our brief fling with mutable summer tasted paradise in a country with certain, unblinking light and heat for nearly half a year.

The demonizing of the Jewish body could have gone no further than our century's version, in which Nazis tried to render dirty Jews into soap for pure Germans, as if we could cleanse them of what they'd done to us. The Nazis hated Jewish ideas, but they hated the Jewish body more. Or they hated Jewish ideas so much they had to annihilate entirely the corporate Jewish body. Thus, the State of Israel's mandate was and continues to be Robert Frost's version of home, "They have to take you in": to be a home for Jewish bodies, still, amazingly enough, under siege in some parts of the world, not only when alive—in Russia, in Syria—but even dead—in cemeteries in France and England, too. When the Jewish body is finally turning to dust, there's still someone capable of degrading it.

\* \* \*

Following a sleepless Friday night of three alarms, my family in Rehovot calls. "How are you doing?" my father's cousin says. "Fine," I tell him, "you?" After the first alarm, he says dryly, *"Tafasti et haprincip"*—I got the idea.

This is the third tale, the sober and confident tale of the people who speak Hebrew, who created this country. Of the God who declared this language holy. And of the mothers who ingeniously covered the floor of their children's plastic tents with candy, so that they would hurry in without complaint. This is the tale I choose to believe in during my war, when I am lauded as a heroine by Israelis I don't know simply for turning up—a fulfillment of my Queen Esther fantasy, that Diaspora narrative of saving the Jews.

Meanwhile, I am holding Joshua in my arms, staring at the plastic tent on that first night. "Get in, Popsky," I say to him. He is crying. His cousins are helping each other put on their masks, but I have disobeyed the instructions of the hotel security staff that I don mine before helping my child; I cannot bring myself to frighten him.

"Get in, sweetie," I say, paralyzed.

"I don't want to," my son cries out, and for a minute literature is mute.

\*    \*    \*

After the Berkeley conference I joined a Hebrew novel-reading group; we meet once a month, and I am the slowest in the class. After a conference on Hebrew in America I started a Hebrew-speaking group. We meet once a week to talk in Hebrew about feminism, psychoanalysis, the crisis of the academy, and all the subjects we wish we could argue about in Hebrew rather than in English with our Israeli friends.

As for the parity with which we met at Berkeley, the mutuality of the Israeli and American Jewish writers is compromised by one indisputable fact: They can read our work in our language; almost none of us can yet read theirs.

\*    \*    \*

*"Tasimi et haben shelakh bifnim"*—put your son inside, someone directs me.

And so Joshua must crawl in, and I must invent stories for him, projected through my mask and his tent in a calm, controlled voice for the hour it takes until the TV announcer says: *"Efshar lihasir et hamaseikhot"*—You can take off your masks.

My great-grandfather said: Yiddish is my mistress, but Hebrew is my wife.

I say: English is my mate, but Hebrew is my lover.

As for my nights in Jerusalem, I cannot translate this experience for anyone.

\*    \*    \*

# Contributors

RUTH ALMOG is a novelist, short-story writer, and author of children's books. Her books include *Margueritas's Nightly Charities, The Exile, After TuBishvat, The Stranger and the Foe, Death in the Rain, Women, The Silver Ball,* and *Roots of Light.* Since 1967, she has been writing for the literary section of *Ha'Aretz.*

MAX APPLE is the author of two novels, *The Propheteers* and *Zip;* two collections of short stories, *Free Agents* and *The Oranging of America,* both awarded the Texas Institute of Letters Award for Best Fiction. He presently teaches at Rice University in Texas, and received a Guggenheim Fellowship in 1987.

HANOCH BARTOV is a novelist and columnist who has published novels, collections of short stories, travel, and military history. Some of his books and various stories were translated into English, Spanish, Russian, and other languages. He is the author of *The Brigade, Whose Little Boy Are You, An Israeli in the Court of St. James, Dado, 48 Years and 20 More Days* (General David Elazar and the Yom Kippur War); and *Mazzal Ayala* and *Yarid Bemoskva* (A Fair in Moscow), published in Hebrew. His latest book, *Zeh Ishl Medaber* (Ishl Speaking), was just published in Hebrew. He is a member of International P.E.N. and President of the P.E.N. Centre in Israel.

CHANA BLOCH, a professor of English at Mills College, is a poet, translator, and critic. She has published two books of poems, *The Past Keeps Changing* and *The Secrets of the Tribe;* a critical study, *Spelling the Word: George Herbert and the Bible;* and three books of translations from Hebrew, *A Dress of Fire: Poems by Dahlia Ravikovitch, Selected Poetry of Yehuda Amichai* (with Stephen Mitchell), and *The Window: New and Selected Poems of Dahlia Ravikovich* (with Ariel Bloch). She has also translated Yiddish Poems by Jacob Gladstein and Abraham Sutzkever, and stories of Isaac Bashevis Singer. Her translation of the Song of Songs (with Ariel Bloch) will be published in 1994.

ROSELLEN BROWN is the author of four novels, *Before and After, Civil Wars, Tender Mercies,* and *The Autobiography of My Mother;* two collections of poetry, *Some Deaths in the Delta* and *Cora Fry; Street Games,* a collection of short stories; and *A Rosellen Brown Reader.* Her stories have been selected six times for the annual anthologies, *O. Henry Prize Stories, The Best American Short Stories,* and *Pushcart Prizes.* She and her husband, Marvin Hoffman, are the authors of a documentary play about the history of anti-Semitism in Russia, *Dear Irina,* produced in Houston in 1987.

ARNOLD EISEN is an Associate Professor of Religious Studies at Stanford University. He is the author of *Galut: Modern Jewish Reflection on Homelessness and Homecoming* and *The Chosen People in America: A Study in Jewish Religious Ideology.*

HILLEL HALKIN is the author of *Letters To An American Jewish Friend,* which was awarded the National Jewish Book Prize in 1977. For thirty years he has been translating classic and contemporary Hebrew authors, including Agnon, Hazaz, Sholom Aleichem, and Amos Oz. He received the Kenneth Smilen Award for the translation of Agnon's *A Simple Story* in 1986.

IRVING HOWE is an author, editor, and critic, and is Emeritus Professor of English at the Graduate Center, City University of New York. His books include *World of Our Fathers, The Critical Point, Decline of the New, Steady Work, Celebrations and Attacks,* his autobiography, *A Margin of Hope,* and a collection of essays, *Socialism and America.* He has translated and edited (with Eliezer Greenberg) *A Treasury of Yiddish Stories, A Treasury of Yiddish Poetry,* and *Voices from the Yiddish.* He has also written critical studies of Thomas Hardy, William Faulkner, and Sherwood Anderson.

ALAN MINTZ is Braun Professor of Modern Hebrew Literature at Brandeis University. He is the author of *Hurban: Responses to Catastrophe in Hebrew Literature, George Eliot and the Novel of Vocation, Banished from their Father's Table: Loss of Faith in Hebrew Autobiography;* and founder and co-editor of *Prooftexts: A Journal of Jewish Literary History.*

AMOS OZ has published fifteen books (novels, short stories, and essays), among them, *In the Land of Israel, Black Box, My Michael, Where the Jackals Howl and Other Stories,* and *To Know A*

*Woman.* His works have been translated into twenty-five languages in over thirty countries. He has received honorary doctorates from Hebrew Union College and Western New England College in Springfield, Massachusetts, and is the recipient of five literary awards, including the Bialik and the Bernstein Prize, and the Prix Femina Etranger—France's top literary award for the best foreign novel of 1988, and the 1992 International Peace Prize of the German Publishers' and Booksellers' Association.

CYNTHIA OZICK is the author of three collections of short stories, *The Pagan Rabbi and Other Stories, Bloodshed and Three Novellas,* and *Levitation and Five Fictions;* four novels, *Trust, The Cannibal Galaxy, The Messiah of Stockholm,* and *The Shawl;* and two collections of essays, *Art & Ardor* and *Metaphor & Memory,* as well as numerous poems, essays, articles, and reviews. She is a translator of Yiddish prose and poetry, including Leivick, Sutzkever, Tabatchnik, and Glatstein. She has received numerous literary awards and her work has been translated into sixteen languages. A play, *Angel,* will be produced in 1993. She was awarded a Jewish Cultural Achievement Award in 1991 from the National Foundation for Jewish Culture.

NESSA RAPOPORT's first novel, *Preparing for Sabbath,* was published by William Morrow & Co. in 1981 and reissued by Biblio Press in 1988. She has now completed her second, *The Perfection of the World.* A collection of her prose-poems, *A Woman's Book of Grieving,* is forthcoming from William Morrow. With Ted Solotaroff she co-edited *Writing Our Way Home: Contemporary Stories by American Jewish Writers,* published by Schocken Books in 1992. Her short stories, essays and articles have appeared widely.

DAVID SCHUETZ is the author of five novels: *The Golden Omary, The Grass and the Sand, I Shall Wait Forever, White Rose, Red Rose,* and *Abishag;* and a collection of short stories, *The Last Chance.* He is a senior producer at the Israel Film Service, and was a recipient of the Prime Minister's Prize in 1982. In 1991, he was awarded the Agnon Literature Prize.

MEIR SHELEV is a columnist for *Yediot Aharonot.* He is the author of *Bible Now: Another Look at Biblical Stories and Figures* and *The Blue Mountain,* which was published in eight countries; and four children's books, *The Monster of Jerusalem, Zohar's Dimples, An Embarrassing Father,* and *Nehama the Louse.* His new novel, *Esau,* published in Israel, has been translated into five languages.

ELI SHALTIEL, historian and editor, is senior editor for non-fiction at Am-Oved Publishers, Tel-Aviv. He has edited and written numerous books and articles, including Moshe Sharrett's *Political Diaries* and Ben Gurion's *Memoirs,* and served as a literary critic for *Ha'aretz* for many years. His book, *Pinhas Rutenberg: 1879–1942, Life and Times* (two volumes) was recently published.

HARVEY SHAPIRO is a poet whose collections include *The Eye, Mountain, Fire, Thornbush, Battle Report, This World, Lauds, Lauds & Nightsounds, The Light Holds,* and *National Cold Storage Company: New and Selected Poems.* He is a deputy editor of *The New York Times Magazine,* having served previously as editor of *The New York Times Book Review.*

RICHARD SIEGEL is Executive Director of the National Foundation for Jewish Culture. He has served as Executive Producer of numerous conferences and productions, including "Independence and Interdependence: Israel–North America Cultural Exchange" of which "The Writer in the Jewish Community" was a part. He is coeditor of *The Jewish Catalog* and *The Jewish Almanac,* and he won the Corporation for Public Broadcasting Award in the Arts and Humanities for the radio production "One People, Many Voices: Jewish Music in America."

TAMAR SOFER was formerly Communications Director for the National Foundation for Jewish Culture. She is now an editor and writer, and has written stories and articles for numerous newspapers and magazines. She was born and raised in Israel, and recently completed her first novel.

TED SOLOTAROFF is a writer and critic. He has edited the critical writings of Isaac Rosenfeld and *Ideas and Issues,* an anthology of prose writing from the sixties. With Nessa Rapoport, he co-edited *Writing Our Way Home: Contemporary Stories by American Jewish Writers*, published by Schocken Books in 1992.

MEIR WIESELTIER has published many volumes of poetry and other writings. He is a founder of Siman Kri'a, the review and publishing house, and has translated Shakespeare, Dickens, Virginia Woolf, Huxley, Brecht, and Lowry into Hebrew. His books include *Jour-*

*ney in Iyona, Chapter A Chapter B, Hundred Poems, Take, Something Optimistic—The Making of Poems,* and *Interior and Exterior, Defectibles,* a collection of poetry translations; *Exit Into the Sea, Poems 1976–1979, The Concise Sixties, Collected Poems Vol. I 1959–1972, A Greek Island, Poems and Prose,* and *Letters and Other Poems, Poems 1980–1986.* He is poetry editor of Am Oved and works on adaptations and new translations of classical plays for the Habima and Cameri theatres.

# Index

153